LET US DRAW NEAR

JUDSON CORNWALL

Judson Cornwall

Heb 10:22

LOGOS INTERNATIONAL
Plainfield, N.J. 07060

SCRIPTURE QUOTATIONS HEREIN
ARE TAKEN FROM THE KING JAMES VERSION
UNLESS OTHERWISE NOTED.

LET US DRAW NEAR
Copyright © 1977 by Logos International
All rights reserved
Printed in the United States of America
International standard book number: 0-88270-226-2
Library of Congress catalog card number: 77-24832
Published by Logos International
Plainfield, New Jersey 07061

ACKNOWLEDGMENTS

My special thanks to Romelle Webber for long hours spent in transcribing my scribbled notes and tired voice into legible manuscript.

The author is deeply indebted to the writings of Arthur W. Pink in *Gleanings in Exodus* published by Moody Press for much of the material in this book. For over thirty years he has ingested these writings, and taught with this book as his outline until it has become part of the warp and woof of his mental fabric. That many of the teachings of this book have come directly, or indirectly, from this association will be obvious to anyone familiar with *Gleanings in Exodus*.

Since my book is not intended to be an exhaustive treatise on the tabernacle, it is strongly recommended that all who desire a more thorough study examine this work for themselves. It has stood the test of time and has much to say to today's generation.

My thanks to Moody Press for their generous permission to quote so freely from this splendid work.

My special thanks to my wife who has endured months of silence as we traveled together, light bulbs burning until the early hours of the morning in tiny motel rooms, and the temptation to become jealous of this book.

PREFACE

The Old Testament devotes fifty chapters to describing the tabernacle and the Book of Hebrews devotes forty-three percent of its content (131 out of 303 verses) to giving us its spiritual meaning. The Holy Spirit is repeatedly trying to teach us principles of heaven. That so few Christians of this twentieth century seem to understand this teaching has motivated me to try to present them afresh.

I have shared portions of the manuscript with a variety of people, and their enthusiastic response goaded me on. Nonetheless, they did have three questions that may very well be in your mind as you read the book. May I answer them for you as I did for them?

1. Could these Old Testament characters really have known so much about God's provision? Perhaps not, but is it fair for us to assume that the Spirit imparted no knowledge until Christ came? Look at the tremendous inspiration of the books in the Old Testament. Would not God have given much revelation, especially at the instigation of the sacrificial system?

2. Haven't you made entering into God's presence too easy? I wonder if the church hasn't made it too hard. The scriptural approach is far simpler than the customary one. As surely as the disciples seemed bent upon keeping people from getting to Jesus, the church seems determined to keep Christians from getting to God.

3. Is this work scholarly enough? I think so. It is honest to the Scripture, based upon years of study on the subject, and the outgrowth of years of teaching the tabernacle. The style is popular but the content is profound. Those spurred on to desire more detailed exposition will find an abundance of more scholarly work available.

If this book will inspire even a handful of believers to come into the full presence of God it will have been worth all of the effort.

To Iverna Tompkins
my beloved sister

Contents

CHAPTER 1

The Prologue

The earth still trembled, but ever so gently compared to the violent shakings of the past month. As far as it is possible to get used to such spectacular phenomena, this multitude of nearly four million people had made the adjustment. Not without apprehension, but with placid resignation.

A few short weeks ago, they had all been slaves; now they were free men. Those terrorizing plagues—who could ever forget them? Then that agonizing visit of the death angel. The memory of the screams and hysteria of the Egyptian masters who lost their first-born had etched itself into the emotions of these people.

Yet all this had led up to their release. In their deep sorrow and mourning, the Egyptians had actually thrust them out of the land, filling their hands with gold and every available item of value. It seemed as though they were trying in one day to atone for national guilt that covered three hundred years of slavery.

Everything had happened so quickly that it was difficult to comprehend it. Far from calculating the worth of their new wealth, they didn't even have time to catalogue it before their leaders called for them to march out of the land that had been their home for at least fifteen generations. It was a move the logistics of which would confuse an army general. There seemed to be so few absolutes and far too many variables for this migration to succeed.

For one thing, where were they going? Up to the moment of departure, their only answer had been "to the promised land," but where and what was that? And since no one had been there, how could they find it? Who would be their guide?

Then there was the matter of food and water. Not only had four million, five hundred thousand people joined in this exodus, they had brought the herds and flocks of Egypt with them. Carrying enough food for them all was impossible, but finding enough to sustain them in the wilderness was unimaginable.

Yet there was an intoxication in being free from slavery—of becoming a nation in their own right—so they followed Moses and Aaron across Goshen. No obstacle seemed insurmountable until they found themselves trapped in the marshlands of the Red Sea with the Egyptian army in hot pursuit.

It was there that the courage born of exuberance evaporated. There was some talk of mutiny against Moses, and many voted to surrender to the Egyptians, preferring a life of slavery to slaughter. They learned that exuberance is easily exhausted during faith's testing time.

Then that pillar of fire dipped between them and the enemy, becoming illumination to them and confusing darkness to the enemy. A spark of hope rekindled their desire for freedom. A strong east wind which blew all night, slicing a pathway through the Red Sea, also produced an increasing faith in this fearful people until by the time the order "forward march" was given, there was no more talk of surrender.

And what a march it was! The water formed huge walls on either side of them, but the pathway was completely dry. Although the swath cut through the sea was wide, it was soon filled with a pulsating mob of people and animals in a seemingly ceaseless wave of motion.

There was no obvious reason for the water to remain piled up as a wall. All past experience would indicate that it should come crashing down at any moment.

But it didn't; not until every person who had dared to come out with Moses had passed through with his cattle and possessions. Then it happened. As the last group of pilgrims reached the far shore, the cloud lifted off the Egyptian camp revealing the deliverance God had wrought for the Hebrews.

How this sight infuriated Pharaoh and his host! They had so smugly rested through the long night assured that these former slaves were trapped and could easily be conquered on the morrow. But by some miracle, they had found a way through the sea.

Although unable to explain it, Pharaoh determined to use this phenomenon to his advantage and issued the command: "Chariots, charge!" Prancing horses pulled the war chariots at top speed into the opened pathway. By now, the dried sea bed was packed hard by the pounding feet of the millions who had passed through so the chariots sped as though traveling on the king's highway.

Fear began to infect the ranks. Well-equipped armies had fled in terror before these trained charioteers. But before the fear could be translated into action, an amazing thing happened. The roadbed in the sea collapsed, miring the chariots up to their hubs and causing many wheels to come off. Before the soldiers could regroup, the walls of water began to collapse. Not one escaped! Their bodies washed up on the shore providing the weapons and armament that these people would need in the months to come.

What rejoicing swept through the crowd as they realized that they would never see their enemy again. The uncertainty and fear gave way to confidence and rejoicing. Miriam grabbed a tambourine and began to lead the women in a dance of rejoicing. Moses hastily composed a song and led the entire group in expressing their enthusiasm in singing. Never had they known such unbridled joy. It was as though they had just been born.

After all God had done for them, what was there to worry about?

3

He was protecting them from the heat with the cloud of His presence, and warming the desert cold with the pillar of fire. This pillar had divided them from their enemies, and was acting as their guide. And now they were on their way to a long-needed vacation—one that God himself was providing. Faith was bubbling like a mountain brook flowing over polished stones.

But for all this effervescence of faith, those stones, however polished, remained in the channel of their hearts. When the singing and dancing were over, the first restriction to faith's flow became evident. They were dangerously low on water. This was something these former residents of the Nile delta had never experienced—thirst. It was a different kind of fear. Death by the sword would have been swift, and by drowning very sure, but death from thirst was slow and uncertain.

When the scouts brought word of a water hole at Marah, there was a temporary halt to the murmuring. But after the water proved to be unpalatably brackish, the murmuring became deafening. There was even talk of revolting against Moses' leadership and returning to Egypt. But before this could get organized, God miraculously sweetened the water by having the elders cast a tree into the pond. It didn't seem too reasonable, but it worked. But then nothing had really made sense for some time. Life had been upset ever since Moses arrived in Egypt proclaiming that Jehovah had sent him to liberate the people from bondage. It had seemed that God was bypassing rational action in favor of supernatural activity. It was hard to identify with Him in it, for this had never been done before, at least not in their recorded history. It created great insecurity in them.

Especially in the provision of manna. This was such an abnormal way to feed people and animals. It couldn't be stored; it had to be gathered fresh daily, and it melted when the dew of the morning evaporated. Would it actually be there each morning? What if they had a night when the temperature remained too high for dew to form? And wouldn't they get tired eating nothing but

4

that white, round, whatever-it-be?

But as with all new things, familiarity breeds confidence, and soon the camp settled into a complacent expectancy of guidance, protection, and provision, however supernatural it had all seemed at the beginning. The abnormal had now become the norm. Not only had the fear abated, but the excitement had waned.

Then it happened. Really happened! They were securely encamped around Mount Sinai enjoying their new life style when the mountain began to belch forth smoke, fire, and noise like an active volcano. The desert shook like a rag in the mouth of a playful puppy. All sense of security vanished instantly. Some declared that it was the end of the world; others just mutely fell to the ground in unconcealed terror. You might have thought that their past experiences would have prepared them for this, but not so.

Even before they could adjust to these new circumstances, a deep, vibrating voice—claiming to be God—spoke from out of the fire declaring that they were God's chosen people. He said that He had done all these miraculous things, and that He intended to make a mighty nation of them. Then He gave some basic instructions for living—about ten specifics—that concerned their attitudes towards God and towards one another.

It was awesome! None had ever heard God's voice, except Moses. Few expected to live through the experience. Urged on by the people, the elders approached Moses asking him to beseech God never to talk audibly to the people again, but to give all His laws and instructions directly to him. They pledged to obey anything God said as long as they did not have to hear it directly from God (Deut. 5:25-27).

Regretfully, Moses acquiesced. He would continue to be their intermediator.

This was well over a month ago. And what a month of insecurity it had been. First Moses and Joshua had taken the elders part way up the mountain with them. The elders came back with a united testimony that they had eaten a meal with God, but Moses and Joshua hadn't come back. Some claimed to be able to see Joshua from time to time standing on a rocky crag of the mountain overlooking the camp just below the base of the fire, but Moses had disappeared into the fire. By now, almost everyone thought that he was dead.

Aaron, the newly appointed leader, submitted to the insistent demands of the people, and molded a golden calf as a visual representation of God. A few called it idolatry, but most felt that they needed something tangible to relate to in worship. Discipline quickly disintegrated during the continued absence of Moses until the fears, anxieties, and long-repressed hostilities erupted into revelry and partying. The unleashed debauchery and lewdness was excused as an expression of worship before the golden calf. Aaron seemed powerless to control the people.

Over the roar of this expressed excitement came the blast of the watchman's trumpet. When the din of the festivities decreased, the watchman's message electrified the people: "Moses is coming down the mountain."

"Moses, alive? Is Joshua with him?"

"Yes!"

How will he react to the changes these past weeks have produced?

They weren't long in finding out, for Moses was in absolute terror! When he saw what was happening, he threw down the two tables of stone upon which God had written the commandments, explaining later that since the commands had already been broken by act, he might as well break them symbolically.

Then he went into dynamic action. Ater he broke up the calf, he burned it, ground it, and threw it on the water supply, making everyone drink it. What a purgative it proved to be!

Even in the midst of his wrath, Moses' face so glowed with God's glory that he put on a veil to spare the people from too severe a confrontation with God's glory.

When Moses called for any who were "on God's side" to join him, most of the tribe of Levi stood with him. They were commissioned to be agents of God's judgment to slay the idolatrous worshipers, and three thousand men were slain that day. What a blood bath!

Once again the camp experienced terror. The God who had delivered them from Egypt's armies and from death by thirst and hunger now had delivered them to death at the hands of their own brethren. Had God spared them just to slay them? Had Moses, their mediator, actually become their murderer?

There was no sleep in the camp that night. The males who survived were busy burying the dead. The widows and bereaved mothers and children were in loud mourning, and the tribe of Levi was in a state of shock.

During this bitter ordeal, Moses called a meeting of the elders. His voice, although somewhat muted by the veil, spoke with authority beyond anything they had ever heard.

"God is displeased with the people's rejection of His voice and presence,"Moses told them, "but He understands their difficulty in being able to relate to Him or to stand in His presence.

"The judgment of today," he continued, "is not for refusing His presence, but for rejecting His word. They had given their solemn pledge to obey anything He told them if He would only withdraw His manifest presence from them and restrict it to me. Yet in the short time I was gone, they already violated the very first things God had said."

"What will be the outcome of all this?" Joshua asked Moses.

"God allowed me to stand between His wrath and these people," he answered. "The sin has been purged and atoned. God's wrath is satisfied. Nothing more will be done, or need be done. This costly sin is behind us now. Our energies must project into the future."

"And just what is that future?" asked Aaron.

"God has declared that He intends to remain among us in spite of the hardness of our hearts,'' Moses reported. "His exact words were: 'And I will set my tabernacle among you: and my soul shall not abhor you. And I will walk among you, and will be your God and ye shall be my people' '' (Lev. 26:11-12).

"How can we handle it if God insists on developing a personal relationship with us?'' Bezaleel queried. "His demonstration on the mountain and His voice devastated all of us. I doubt if we could live through a repeat performance. Why, even with all the preparation you gave us, we elders were not ready for what we experienced on the lower slope of the mount with you and God. How could we ever get used to living with God in our midst?''

"God has a plan,'' Moses remarked. "He asks that we build Him a portable dwelling to be erected in the middle of the camp. It is to have three compartments: an outer court where the people can come to worship, a holy place where the priests can worship, and a most holy place where God will reside.

"God has promised to dwell in His compartment,'' Moses explained, "thereby remaining unthreatening to the worshiper. He will confine His voice to this most holy place, and only those commissioned to enter will ever confront His presence, or hear His voice.''

"But who would ever dare enter even the holy place, much less the most holy place?'' Aaron asked.

Shifting the uncomfortable veil to another position on the bridge of his nose, Moses answered, "God has chosen a priesthood to represent the people unto Him and Him unto the people. Annually the high priest will come before Jehovah to make atonement for their sins. To qualify him to make this entrance, God has provided seven stations of worship—or seven pieces of furniture for His tabernacle. Each one effects certain changes in the believer-priest.

"Two of these pieces of furniture are to be placed in the outer court,'' he continued, "while three of them are to be in the holy place, with the final two in the most holy place. Their placement will form a cross visible in its entirety only to God.''

8

How can pieces of furniture change a man into a creature who can stand and enjoy the presence of God?'' Joshua asked.

"Well," Moses continued, "first of all, each piece offers a progressive revelation of God and His nature. The material out of which it is constructed, the dimensions, and its usage all make God more meaningful and understandable. Additionally, as the priest ministers at each station, he will find himself being changed 'from faith to faith' and 'from glory to glory.' God has chosen this method both to reveal himself and to change His man."

"When do we start?" one of the elders asked.

"I must return to the mount to get the full plans. The sin of the people interrupted God's revelation. When I return, I'll have the full blueprints plus a list of the workmen God has chosen to oversee the construction.

"There is, nevertheless, one part of God's plan that could be implemented during my absence, for God has designated an exact order for the encampment of His people that will make room for His special tabernacle to be placed exactly at the center of the camp. I have shared the plan with Aaron already. Help him set it up as quickly as possible.

"Brethren, retain divine order in the camp until I return with the divine ordinances and the plans for the tabernacle. And may 'The LORD bless thee, and keep thee: The LORD make his face shine upon thee, and be gracious unto thee: The LORD lift up his countenance upon thee, and give thee peace' " (Num. 6:24-26).

With these closing words of benediction, Moses left the tent and headed for another confrontation with God in the mountain.

That early dawn, as the elders watched him ascend the stony path he had already climbed twice before, this time carrying tables of stone to replace the two he had broken earlier, they felt a surging stream of excitement and anticipation. God was going to make it possible for them to stand the living presence of His glory as He had done for their leader Moses. A fresh revelation of God was coming that would forever remove the terrorizing fear of His

9

presence. If they had known how, they would have started construction of the tabernacle that very day; but, since they didn't, they began to discuss the new encampment procedures with the heads of the tribes. The adjustment would nearly equal a move, but it would keep the people occupied during Moses' absence and might very well prevent another revolt against God. Besides this, if they could have it completed before the return of Moses with the plans, they could begin to build the tabernacle almost immediately.

THE ENCAMPMENT.

CHAPTER 2

The Outer Court

EXODUS 27:9-19

It was a far different sight that greeted Moses as he descended from the high crag the next time. The sounds of revelry had been replaced with serenity, and the frenzied merrymaking had given way to orderliness. The purging had been effective.

But the sight of the totally rearranged camp was breath-taking as Moses descended below the cloud of God's presence and got a panoramic view of the camp site. He set down the box he was carrying and its precious contents, the rewritten commandments, to take it all in. There in the center of the camp was the wide open space where they would erect the tabernacle just as soon as they could build it. The compass points of the camp had been signified with the banners of the four chosen tribes. Due east, where the gate to the outer court would be placed, was Judah's insignia of a lion. Opposite it, to the west, was Ephraim's banner with the picture of an ox on it, while Dan's standard with the eagle marked the northern compass point, and Reuben's was positioned due south with the face of a man on his banner. Is it possible that God had allowed Moses to see these as the four faces of the cherubim as Ezekiel would later see (Ezek. 10:14)?

Even so, it is highly improbable that he would know that these four standards beautifully picture the four Gospels which would be written to share the life of Christ Jesus about whom every detail of the tabernacle speaks. Matthew, showing Christ as king, answers to the lion. Mark, revealing Christ as the servant, is a natural for the ox. Luke portrays Jesus as the man, and John unfolds Him as the Son of God, the eagle. Little wonder, then, that God had chosen these four tribes to establish the directions by which the entire camp would pitch.

But it was not merely the orderliness of having the camp pitch to the compass points instead of setting up ''catch-as-catch-can'' fashion that overwhelmed Moses. Even he had not realized that when God instructed him to place the smallest tribes to the west, and the largest tribes to the east, while the tribes to the north and south were nearly equal in number, it would form a gigantic living cross of millions of people and their black goats' hair tents.

God's place would be at the intersection of this cross, and the people would be in the cross with Him. Moses sat down next to the box, which would later become the ark of the covenant, and gave himself time to take it all in, for he knew that once he got into the camp, he would be unable to see the massive cross. It had to be viewed from above.

Little wonder, then, that in the months to come when Balaam was ready to curse God's people, he was unable to do so. No matter what mountain peak he would ascend, he would see Israel's camp as a great cross. There can be no curse placed upon a people who live in the cross with Christ in their midst.

''Moses, Moses, is that you?''

It sounded like the voice of Joshua who had once again pitched a tent midway up the mountain to wait for Moses.

''Yes, Joshua. Come on up. You need to see what I am seeing.''

Although Joshua had watched the rearranging of the camp from his tent and during his exercise periods, he had not been high enough to see the camp as Moses was seeing it.

''Oh, Moses, it's spectacular,'' Joshua said, as he lowered

himself to sit with Moses and catch his breath from the rapid climb. "What does it mean?"

"In the mountain God spoke of a coming redeemer who would be killed upon a cross shaped similar to this. They will fasten him on it and then erect it in the earth. He is to be God's sacrifice for sin. By having us camp in the shape of a cross and by arranging the tabernacle furniture to form a cross, God is constantly reminded that atonement for His people is assured through substitutionary sacrifice."

"Is fellowship with man really worth such a price?" Joshua asked.

"God seems to think so," Moses answered.

"Then why do the people so completely reject this intimate relationship with God?" Joshua said.

"Because of fear," Moses said. "Fear of the unknown is a potent power inherent in each of us. But God's answer to this is to cause us to come to know Him through a revelation of himself and to replace our fear with love."

"But," Joshua interrupted, "how can God reveal himself to us when the people refuse to let Him speak again? They fear that hearing His voice will destroy them."

"I know," Moses replied. "I asked God that very same question. He said that since they would not hear His voice or accept a demonstration of His nature, He would speak to them through symbols, types, and shadows. That is the main purpose of the tabernacle. Everything in it is designed to reveal some facet of God. The materials used, the dimensions, the colors, and even the positioning of the furniture all proclaim something about God and His coming Christ. God is planning to reveal himself to us through picture language."

Both men silently stared at the massive encampment that filled the desert valley below them. It was barely an hour past sunrise but already the hustle and bustle of activity was discernable. The women were headed towards the outskirts of the camp with their

15

manna pots deftly balanced on their heads. They had to reach the manna fields before the dew evaporated.

Several times Joshua attempted conversation, but seemed unable to put his thoughts into words. Although his eyes seemed fixed on the camp, he wasn't seeing anything, really. He was lost in contemplation of the promised graphic portrayal of the God he loved and worshiped.

"It is overwhelming, isn't it?" Moses said in a half-whisper. "God is going to live in the midst of that encampment down there."

"Are you certain, Moses?" Joshua asked.

"He promised me: 'I will set my tabernacle among you: and my soul shall not abhor you. And I will walk among you, and will be your God, and ye shall be my people' " Moses said, reassuringly (Lev. 26:11-12).

Moments later a wild goat, foraging for something to eat, rounded the boulder which had hidden the men from its view, and stopped, momentarily frozen in its tracks. They could almost see him tuning his senses to a fine pitch while assessing the danger level. Moses and Joshua didn't even bat an eyelash while silently staring back at this ram. With a sharp snort, the goat made a flying leap, half sideways, and disappeared in the rough terrain many feet below Moses.

"I'm afraid that's what the people will do when they are confronted by God," Joshua said. "We didn't give that goat any cause for fear, and yet after one quick look, he fled the scene as though we were hungry hunters."

"That's why God plans to shut himself away from the people's view," Moses said. "Not only will He be in the innermost court of the sanctuary, but He has provided that a curtain wall be placed around the three courts.

"Try to picture this, Joshua," he continued. "In the very center of that open space in the midst of the camp, we will erect a fence of white linen about seven and one-half feet high, one hundred fifty

16

feet long, and seventy-five feet wide. It will be suspended on rods hung between sixty posts. This will assure the campers that God will not come bursting out on them. It will also afford privacy for those who do choose to approach God in the outer court. They will be able to confess their sins and offer their sacrifice unrestrained by the gaze and eavesdropping of their neighbors.''

"Its obvious purpose, then," Joshua said, "is separation. It will isolate the profound from the profane; the sacred from the secular, won't it?''

"I understood from God," Moses said, "that this pictures the righteousness of the coming Messiah (white linen) that shuts the world out and also shuts the believer in with God. Righteousness is not a price the believer must pay; it is a protection he receives when he approaches God in the prescribed way. Anyone unwilling to be encompassed by the righteousness of the Messiah can never be a worshiper and draw near to God. He clearly said: 'Holiness, without which no man shall see the Lord' (Heb. 12:14). I suppose, Joshua, that to the spectator remaining in the camp, the wall will seem awesome and prejudiced; but to the worshiper and the priest it will be beautiful. We can, 'Worship the LORD in the beauty of holiness' (Psa. 29:2).

"God called this enclosure 'the tent of the congregation' (Exod. 39:40), for this is the appointed place of assembly and worship for the people. None but the priests can come any closer to God. God will meet with the priests in the holy place, but with the people in the outer court.''

"How beautifully it speaks of the coming Messiah as the meeting place between God and His people," Joshua added.

In years to come, John would write: "And the Word [Christ] became flesh (human, incarnate) and tabernacled—fixed His tent of flesh, lived awhile—among us; and we [actually] saw His glory—His honor, His majesty . . ." (John 1:14, TAB).

Moses stood up, stretched his arms high above his head, and

17

yawned. He was beginning to feel tired after those long days in the presence of God. He couldn't remember how long it had been since he had enjoyed a full night's sleep. There had been so much to learn; so many laws to write down, that he had existed on cat naps for the past month.

Reaching for the box so that he could resume his journey downward, Moses had to insist that Joshua not carry it for him. "It is designed to be carried by more than one person. Let's share the burden the rest of the way home," he said.

Silently they picked their footing on the pathless climb down the mountain. Each seemed to be lost in his own meditation about God's provision to live in their midst.

"Moses," Joshua said, breaking a long silence, "the court for worship seems incredibly small for so many people, doesn't it? I calculate that the entire enclosure wouldn't be much over thirty seven hundred yards square."

"It's smaller than you think," Moses answered, "when you consider that nearly half of that enclosure will be taken up with the tabernacle structure itself, and that the remaining eighteen hundred square yards must accommodate the brazen altar, the laver, the cattle pens, the choir and orchestra, as well as the worshipers."

"The court will be so crowded with people that the priests won't have room to work," Joshua said. "There is no other place the people will be allowed to worship."

"Those were my thoughts," Moses said, "but God assured me that the court would rarely, if ever, be filled to capacity. It seems that God really doesn't expect very many of those he has freed, led, and fed to come into His presence to worship. He says that the vast majority of them will be content to live under His protection and in His provision without ever becoming involved with His presence. The worshipers will be a 'little flock' (Luke 12:32) in the midst of the greater flock. Only a few will choose the 'narrow way' (Matt. 7:14) of the outer court of worship."

"Why, then, has God reserved such a large portion of land for

His tabernacle if the court is to be so small?'' Joshua asked.

"Because the tribe of Levi came to my aid in defending the holiness of God in the matter of the golden calf last month,'' Moses explained, "God has chosen them to be ministers in the tabernacle and helpers to the priests. They will pitch their tents between the curtained fence and the tents of the congregation on the north, the south, and the west. Aaron and you and I and our families will pitch our tents to the east of the court. It will afford the people further separation from God, but will make access to God much easier for those who will daily minister unto the Lord and His service.''

"Those who serve continually abide closely,'' Joshua mused.

Little more was said for the remainder of the descent. The box, with its tables of stone, written laws, and full plans for the tabernacle, seemed to grow heavier with each step. Several times they had to rest, but even then they didn't engage in conversation.

Moses was preparing himself mentally to meet with the elders and to accept the weight of responsibility he knew would press on his shoulders the moment he entered the camp.

Joshua was lost in the wonder of the revelation of the Messiah that had come to him in merely talking about the tabernacle. What would it actually be like after it was constructed and God had moved in?

Children playing at the base of the mountain first spotted them. Running at what seemed to be breakneck speed, they more screamed than called, "Moses and Joshua—Moses and Joshua are back!'' Within a few minutes, most of the camp was aware of the joyous return of their leader.

Younger hands eagerly relieved Moses and Joshua of their burden, and the throng of well-wishers quickly enlarged to a full crowd of people, all talking and asking questions simultaneously.

When he got to the door of his tent, Moses greeted his tearful wife and his sons. He would never understand why women wept as an expression of happiness.

Joshua busied himself with nothing, trying desperately to give Moses a few moments of privacy with his family; yet he didn't want to let him out of his sight, for in this man Moses, and in him alone, lay all of Israel's hope of building a residence for God among them.

"Joshua!" Moses called. "Assemble the elders in the tent of meeting at high noon. I don't want to lose another day in getting started on the plans."

Excitedly, Joshua set out on his errand while Moses stepped into his tent to enjoy his first home-cooked meal in a month and a half.

The normally sedate elders sat on the carpeted floor of the tent excitedly talking about the things Joshua had reported to them. It sounded far more like a marketplace when the caravans arrived than an official meeting of the ruling body of all Israel. But then, the meeting had not officially commenced. So great was the excitement that everyone had arrived early. Their anticipation of Moses' arrival was electric. They had so much to report to him, and so very much to learn from him!

A young lad, a self-assigned watchman for the elders, slapped his bare feet increasingly fast on the sandy pathway leading to the tent as he breathlessly called: "Moses is coming; he's almost here." Forgetting his manners, he rushed inside the tent, face ablaze with excitement, and almost rudely re-announced: "I said, Moses is coming."

Like their marketplace at sundown on Fridays, the conversation dwindled to a hushed silence in an amazingly short period of time.

"Be gone, boy!" one of the elders whispered, gesturing with the back of his hand.

As he made his exit he held the tent flap open, for Moses was almost ready to walk in. As Moses entered, all of the elders stood to their feet in respect. Moses was radiant with the glory of God, just as he had been the last time he came down from the presence of God. It was awesome, but attractive. There was a gentleness and a peace that seemed to accompany him that reassured the elders that

20

all was well.

Moses lovingly greeted each of the seventy elders with a hug and a kiss, and then led them in a responsive prayer of thanksgiving.

The men again seated themselves in a semicircle, all facing Moses. Their excitement spilled over in noisy chatter and hand clapping until one of them, completely overwhelmed with joy, broke out singing the song Moses had composed and taught them after their victorious passage through the Red Sea some months earlier. The rest of the elders joined him on the second verse singing lustily, as only men in times of great elation can sing:

> The LORD is my strength and song,
> And he is become my salvation:
> He is my God, and I will prepare him an habitation;
> My father's God, and I will exalt him (Exod. 15:2).

In response to this joyous outburst in song, Moses reached over to his brother, Aaron, whispered briefly in his ear, and the two of them stood up and sang, as a duet, still another verse of that song:

> Thou in thy mercy hast led forth
> The people which thou hast redeemed:
> Thou hast guided them in thy strength
> Unto thy holy habitation (Exod. 15:13).

"Moses," Eldad, the senior member of the council of elders, said, "we have done all that you requested us to do. The camp has been totally reorganized, the repentance of the people seems to be complete, and we have shared with them what you told us about building a tabernacle for God to dwell in."

"And they're enthusiastic about it," broke in Nahshon, captain of Judah. "Everyone is willing to give and do anything God requires of us."

"Excellent," Moses said. "We're going to need a large supply of gold, silver, brass, blue, purple, scarlet, fine linen, goats' hair, rams' skins dyed red, badgers' skins, acacia wood, oil for the light, spices for the anointing oil and for sweet incense, onyx stones, and other precious stones to be set in the breastplate (Exod. 25:3-7).

"It may take us a few months to fell the trees and cut the lumber," Nethaneel, captain of Issachar, said, "but the rest of the materials can be collected in just a few days. The people are rich with the gifts that the Egyptians thrust on them the night of the passover, and they're eager to give much of it back to God."

"Now, Moses, please tell us about the plans God gave you for the tabernacle," Aaron said.

Hour after hour, Moses continued to talk about God's wonderful tabernacle. He told them that it was patterned after the heavens and that he had repeatedly been warned to build it according to the pattern he was shown on the mount. Moses gave exact dimensions for everything, and even briefly discussed the method of construction to be used. He emphasized that everything had to be portable so the construction would be a combination of modular and knockdown type. Nothing could be larger than an oxcart could haul.

Although they knew they could not remember all of these facts, the elders were so excited to hear the details that they sent out for lamps at sundown rather than breaking for the night. It seemed that every man had at least a dozen questions he wanted to ask, but Moses didn't want to field questions until he had completely covered the subject.

Moses asked Joshua to explain what he had taught him on the mount about the cross-shaped encampment, the curtained wall, the reason for the smallness of the court, and the positioning of the tribe of Levi.

About the time that Joshua had finished with his subject, the lamps arrived. To their delight, when their wives realized that this meeting was going to go into the night, they had hastily pooled their manna supplies and prepared their evening meal "to go." This fellowship knit their hearts together even more firmly, for they had not dined as a group since they all ate with God at the lower limit of the mountain just after the commandments had been given, some three months before.

It was well after dark before Moses opened the session to questions.

"I'm disturbed at the style of construction," Eliab, who was captain of the tribe of Zubulun, said. "We know the building trade well enough; haven't we built Pharaoh enough cities over the years? But we are artisans in bricks and stone. We've always built massive, permanent structures. Who among us knows how to work in wood and gold, or how to construct a portable structure that may have to be disassembled and reassembled many times in the years to come?"

"God told me that He would impart special knowledge to many of the men of the congregation. Some will discover that they know how to do one thing, and others will find abilities in other fields. God is going to let us build it for Him, but He will impart the necessary knowledge through His Spirit," Moses answered.

"But Moses," Elizur, captain of Reuben, asked, "who among us can supervise such construction? You're the only one who really understands the plans, and you're already overworked. Surely you don't intend to supervise this project too, do you?"

"No," Moses responded, "I don't. I am needed in too many other areas to become the builder, but God told me who would be the construction superintendent. God has already imparted the special wisdom he will need to supervise this project. Bezaleel, son of Uri of the tribe of Judah, stand up! You are God's chosen superintendent, and God has given you Aholiab, son of Ahisamach, of the tribe of Dan, as your assistant" (Exod. 31).

Bezaleel hesitantly rose to his feet. Incredulity slowly gave way to amazement in his mind as he pondered these words. He, of all the men of Israel, would supervise the construction of God's dwelling place. Is this why he had sensed such an absorbing interest in the details of Moses' report? Perhaps this explained why he seemed to understand many details that the others had questioned Moses about. Maybe God was already giving him understanding.

23

Applause interrupted his thoughts, and he modestly bowed to the elders in response. How different this was from the years of slavery where he had supervised much of the working in gold and silver in the Egyptian temples, but always under duress and fear. Now he had been commanded to an even greater work; not through an intimidating whip, but by an anointing from God and the approval of his brethren.

The appearance of his oldest son caused Moses to close the session for the evening. "After all," he said, "my children have hardly seen me in three months. You brethren can begin to gather the materials we will need from each of the tribes. Let there be no compulsion; God wants His abode to be constructed from freewill offerings.

"We'll meet here again in three days, shortly after sunrise. Be ready to report on the offerings at that time."

Grasping the right hand of his just-appointed assistant, Aholiab, and reaching for Joshua's hand to his right, Bezaleel began to sing again the song of Moses. The rest of the elders joined him as soon as they realized what he was doing:

> The LORD is my strength and song,
> And he is become my salvation:
> He is my God, and I will prepare him an habitation;
> My father's God, and I will exalt him.

Reluctantly, they took their leave. It seemed that each one wanted to be the last to go.

SOUTHEAST VIEW OF THE TABERNACLE.

CHAPTER 3

The Tabernacle

EXODUS 26

Joshua arrived at Moses' tent before his wife got back from gathering the daily supply of manna. His youthful embarrassment couldn't hide the obvious anticipation on his face. "We meet with the elders again today," he said, half apologetically, "and I thought I would walk over with you."

"Oh, the eagerness and enthusiasm of youth," Moses thought to himself. How well he remembered his own impetuous youth. He had often stirred the court of Pharaoh to anger and resentment, and to his dying day he would remember how his burning zeal had caused him to commit murder. But then, forty years alone in the desert had taken most of that out of him. A few more years would mellow Joshua, too. He probably needed to take a wife to help mature him further. Zipporah had certainly been a tool of God to aid in his own maturation.

"You'll join us for breakfast, won't you?" Zipporah asked as she stepped into the tent.

"That's the best offer I've had today," Joshua responded. "Besides, no one in Israel can fix manna better than you."

Zipporah recognized the flattery, but liked it. Moses was loving and gracious, but since he had met God at the burning bush, he always seemed to be preoccupied and extremely serious. She smiled as she stepped outside the tent to hurriedly prepare Moses' breakfast, for she knew that inside that calm exterior was a man eager to get started on the construction of the tabernacle. He had been with her and the children for three days now, but she could tell that his mind had been elsewhere most of the time. Oh how she wished she still had him all to herself back tending her father's sheep instead of leading this mob of ex-slaves. But she would make the best of it, for she knew the change in Moses had been by divine appointment, not by Moses' choice.

She served the men their meal as elegantly and pleasantly as she knew how. Not that they noticed. They were so engrossed in discussing the tabernacle.

Talking all the way, Moses and Joshua walked leisurely to the scheduled meeting with the elders, a mongrel dog preceding them noisily. From time to time, he circled back to them to see what was taking them so long and urged them to hurry, while Moses rubbed the scruff of his neck as if to say, "Don't rush me, boy, we've got a long day ahead of us."

Although Moses had called for this assembly of the elders to be held at the tent of meeting, the elders had requested that it be moved to the tabernacle site for people had been standing in line for nearly three days bringing their construction gifts, and all the elders had been pressed into service to sort and store the materials.

Since Moses had not been home long enough to move his tent, it was still quite some distance from the site, and he had not been aware of the intense activity of these past three days. But one look at the area told the story. Although it was only an hour after sunrise, already there were long lines of people with furs draped over their shoulders, or gold and silver implements in their hands, or great bolts of linen cloth carried between husband and wife. It reminded him of tax-collecting days back in Egypt, except that there was no murmuring. Instead, there were the unmistakable sounds of hilarity as they sang, shouted, spoke joyfully one to another, and even did an occasional dance of exuberance. Clearly, the people wanted to build God a place of habitation, no matter what it might cost them. The elders had obviously done a good job of communicating with the people.

Seeing Moses and Joshua approaching, Bezaleel walked out to meet them. "The people bring much more than enough for the service of the work, which the LORD commanded to make," he said (Exod. 36:5).

So Moses ordered runners to go throughout the camp to tell the people that there was no need to bring further offerings, for what they had already given was more than sufficient, and even too much (Exod. 36:7).

"As far as I can tell right now," Bezaleel reported, "we are only short on timber and linen. However, we have more than enough flax to weave the additional linen we need."

"Excellent," Moses said, "for that will get the women involved in the construction. Choose out the finest weavers from among them and have them weave the three hangings that will form the doorways to the three courts and the outer court walls. The women can also do much of the embroidery work on these curtains and on the linen ceiling for the tabernacle, as well as make the priestly garments."

"May I suggest," Bezaleel answered, "that Miriam, your sister, be placed in charge of the weaving, for she is good at the loom, and the women deeply love her. And how about putting Zipporah, your wife, over those who will do the fancy needlework? She is skillful with the needle and highly respected by the women because of you. I suppose that Aaron's wife would be the natural choice for supervising the sewing of the priestly garments."

"I have placed the construction in your hands," Moses responded, "you choose your own workmen."

"Thank you for your confidence, Moses," Bezaleel said. "I have given considerable thought to just how to select the workmen.

Since my assistant's name means 'The Tabernacle of the Father,' I thought it would be logical to put Aholiab in charge of the construction of the tabernacle itself—the tent structure. My next idea had been to assign the work by tribes with the captain of the tribe in charge of a specific area of construction, but I have thought better of it. I fear that in days to come there could be tribal pride in the portion they built instead of identification with the whole, so I have decided to mix workmen from each tribe on every major construction project. I believe we will soon discover the ones God has endowed with particular wisdom for the various tasks.

"If it meets with your approval, I suggest that we not have you or the Levites move your tents to this open area until after all construction is completed. This will give us a large working area and will make my job of supervision much easier."

"My spirit agrees with all of your suggestions, and I am thankful that I do not have to move right away. Besides, the noise of the construction would greatly interfere with our home life. Zipporah will be glad to escape that," Moses said, "and so will all of the priestly families."

"I have studied the blueprints you brought down from the mountain almost day and night since you returned," Bezaleel said, "and I am amazed at how well I seem to understand the construction techniques needed to build it. But I must admit that I certainly do not understand why it is being built just as it is. I can see many areas that could be greatly simplified, and other places where I think a simple change would make it even more efficient."

Somewhat alarmed, Moses said, "Don't you dare change even one small detail of those plans! Repeatedly, God charged me to be certain everything was constructed exactly according to the plan given to me on the mount. You see, everything has a typical meaning; all is a foreshadowing of the coming Messiah. If we dare alter the type, it will give a false picture of the true. Jehovah told me that the same Spirit that is anointing you to comprehend the plans will enable you and the workmen to construct everything designated in them, and furthermore, He will also teach you the meaning of everything you build. Listen to the gentle voice within you during the hectic months ahead, for 'He will guide you into all truth . . . and He will shew you things to come' '' (John 16:13).

It was late in the afternoon before things calmed down enough that a united discussion could be held. Although their enthusiasms were still unbounded, the magnitude of the task before them produced some very sober conversation among the elders.

"We'll need to construct a small furnace or smelter to melt down the gold and silver articles," one said.

"And anvils and hammers to beat it into sheets thin enough to overlay the wood," added another.

"Someone will have to make a very strong glue to use in laminating the boards. The entire tabernacle uses boards twenty-seven inches wide and there aren't many trees here in this area that can give us that size board," chimed in still another.

"And we'll need a lot of leather lacing cut from the skins to use in sewing together the skin coverings for the main tent."

And so it went for the rest of the day. Elder after elder had questions and suggestions on how to get the work going.

Bezaleel didn't try to answer the questions; he merely noted the suggestions and the wisdom of the questioner. It was becoming obvious to him that he and Aholiab were not going to construct God a house, they would merely oversee the work. This holy habitation would be built by the entire body of Israel working together. This was good. Up to then, everything had been done for them, now it was to be done by them. May God be praised!

The days that followed flowed one into another. The tabernacle site looked like a beehive during the blossom season; people coming and going, bringing and taking away in ceaseless activity. The happy noises almost sounded like a hymn of praise.

The original confusion and competition soon gave way to cooperation and completion. Much of the work was done on assembly lines which speeded the development of expertise.

31

While awaiting the arrival of the first timber, the metal workers were beating gold into thin plates for overlaying and began casting silver foundation blocks and hooks. Others were smelting brass for use in the outer court and forged the pans, hooks, shovels, snuffers, etc., which would be needed to perform the service of the tabernacle.

At the other side of the work site, men stirred great vats of steaming red dye filled with rams' skins which were then spread out on the sand to dry.

The spinning, the weaving, the cutting, and the sewing were done in special tents erected to protect the white linen from the dust of all the other activities.

Although the work pace was swift, there was no sense of haste. There were no deadlines to meet and no quotas to fill. It was a labor of love and was performed in a relaxed atmosphere of joviality. What a contrast it was to their work schedule in Egypt, and yet Egypt's whips had taught them the discipline to work.

As a result, there were no slowdowns or slacking in pace so that within months, they could begin erecting the tabernacle itself.

By prior agreement, the sabbath before the first assembling of materials into a building was proclaimed a day holy unto the Lord. A solemn assembly was called, and the people fasted from sunup to sundown and then enjoyed a feast of greater magnitude than anything they had ever done since they came out of Goshen. The anticipation of seeing all of their individual efforts blend into one structure was released exuberantly. The jubilee lasted far into the night, so Moses wisely declared the following two days as days of rest.

On Tuesday, when the Levites arrived, they found that Bezaleel and Aholiab had already stretched lines marking the foundation outline and were beginning to place the silver sockets, or foundation blocks, in place, two for each board. No gold was to touch the earth. It had to rest on silver, which speaks of redemption. All manifestation of divine glory (gold) must rest

32

upon the redemptive work of Christ (silver) in order to be revealed to mankind (earth). Upon these ninety-six silver sockets rested the whole fabric of the tabernacle, for redemption is the only basis on which Christ becomes the meeting place between a holy God and His innately sinful people. Since reconciliation rests upon redemption by ransom, the silver that formed these sockets had come from the "atonement money" (Exod. 30:16) with which the Hebrews had redeemed their first-born sons.

. Into the hand-like "tenons," which fit into the foundation sockets, sat the acacia planks. The Greek version of the Old Testament translates it "incorruptible wood." How beautifully it typifies the real and untainted manhood of the Lord Jesus. Grown on the earth and formed from materials in the earth, yet indestructible, incorruptible; able to withstand the ravishings of weather and the passage of time. Through the incarnation, the Lord Jesus became spotless and perfect humanity. But none of the wood could be seen in these planks that were two and one-third feet wide and fifteen feet long, for they had been completely overlaid with gold. It was never the human nature of Jesus that was seen in the tabernacle (wood), it was always the divine nature of Christ (gold), for this was being erected as a type of the heavenlies.

The planks were placed standing up (Exod. 26:15), not lying down; that is, vertical, not horizontal. While we are all *fallen* creatures, Christ Jesus was upright in all His ways.

"Shift that plank just a little to the right until it is touching the other one. That's right. Now straighten it up," Aholiab instructed. "I believe we'd better have two men hold it in place; one on the outside, and the other on the inside, until we can get the connecting bars in place. You sons of Merari of the tribe of Levi (Num. 3:36) will be assembling and disassembling this building for many years to come, so we might as well find the smoothest method right from the beginning."

By this time, eight other men were carrying the third plank from the pile to be erected in a straight line with the previous two. The

33

north and south sides would each have twenty of these boards and the back wall, to the west, would have a total of eight; two of them, however, would be corner boards to increase the stability of the structure.

"All right now," Aholiab called, "bring that scaffold over here so we can reach the top rings and slip the connecting bars into place. Careful, now . . . that should do it. Now bring one of the bars over here. No, not the long one, that goes the full length through the middle sockets. Bring one of the shorter bars. It will extend half the length. Fine. Now slip it through the rings. Good. Now move the scaffold down to the other end and do the same thing."

Methodically, Aholiab called out instructions as though he had supervised construction such as this all of his life. The Levites were amazed at how smoothly everything was going, especially since they had never done anything like this before.

By noon, all forty-eight boards had been put into place and anchored with the gold-covered wooden bars. Also, the pillars and bars were set in place in the center of the tabernacle to support the veil, and in the front end upon which the tabernacle door would hang. It was an amazingly rigid structure, totally self-supporting. And well it must be, for upon these golden boards would rest all of the weight of the curtains and coverings, just as on the God-man was hung all of the weight of the divine government and all of the glories of His Father's house. The responsibility of the revelation of God's presence and glory always pressed down upon Christ Jesus.

When the last Levite scampered down from the scaffolding, the crowd of spectators broke into a long and loud applause. Compared to their black goats' hair tents, these golden walls, about fifteen feet wide and forty-five feet long, looked magnificent. They glistened in the sun like a giant harvest moon transposed to the desert floor. Never again would they see it as just now, for the walls of the outer court would hide much of the

34

construction from their view once all was completed. And before the tabernacle would be used, it would be totally covered with skins. Only the priests, who had access to the inside, would see these radiant golden walls after this, for God's glory is seen by the worshiper who comes into His presence, not by the spectator who looks on from a distance.

Because it was important that all of the coverings be put in place at one time to protect the curtained ceiling, Aholiab suggested that they call it a day. "May you sons of Merari, encamped to the north of the tabernacle, always handle this portion of the tabernacle that has been given to your charge with care and respect," he told them as he dismissed them.

In the meantime, he chose some volunteers from the spectators to carry the linen curtains from the tents where they had been prepared to the interior of the tabernacle walls and instructed them to cover them with badger skins.

In the orientation session on Wednesday morning, Aholiab told the sons of Gershon, of the tribe of Levi, to whom God had committed the responsibility for the curtains and hangings of the tabernacle (Num. 3:25), "The ceiling of the tabernacle, as you know, will be composed of ten white curtains, each one forty-two feet long and six feet wide. Before we raise them, we will couple them together in fives, width to width, giving us two pieces about forty-two feet by thirty feet. We will stretch one of these from the front of the tabernacle and bring the other one up from the back side, meeting at the middle about where the veil will hang. You realize, of course, that this not only forms the ceiling, but totally covers the outside of the boards on all sides."

"It seems to be an extra fine linen," one of the Levites said. "Isn't it apt to be rather fragile?"

"You're right, it isn't the same coarse linen we will be using for the walls of the outer court. This is a picture of the manifested holiness and righteousness of the coming Messiah. The three colors used for embroidering the cherubim upon it all have typical meanings that are precious. The blue speaks of His celestial origin, the purple is emblematic of His royalty, while the scarlet speaks of the sufferings of the Messiah. You priests will be constantly made aware that side by side with His purity, His heavenly character, and His royal majesty, the Messiah will be a suffering Savior bearing the iniquity of man and the wrath of God."

Gently, the men worked the curtains into position and inched them toward each other until the fifty blue loops on the edge of one curtain overlapped the fifty blue loops on the other one. They could hardly fail to see a relationship between the two sets of five curtains and the two sets of five commandments placed on stones. The first five define man's responsibility Godward and are joined together by the words, "The Lord thy God," and the last five commandments define man's responsibility manward and do not contain the words, "The Lord thy God." In forming the ceiling with ten curtains grouped together in two sets of fives, there is an obvious picture of Christ, as the representative of His people, meeting the whole of their obligations both Godward and manward. He, and He alone, loved God with all His heart, and His neighbor as himself.

"Bring the gold couplings," Aholiab called, "and pass one through each pair of loops to unite the curtains together."

It is only we on this side of the coming of Christ who can really understand the meaning of coupling the two curtains together with golden clasps, for it is when we read the record of His life that we see how the divine manifestation (gold) enabled Christ to combine and perfectly adjust the claims of God and the needs of man without ever marring the unity of His character. We see His inflexible righteousness and then His exceeding tenderness; His uncompromising faithfulness in denouncing hypocrisy and then the wondrous compassion for poor sinners; His stern denunciation of error and human traditions, and then the tender patience toward the ignorant and those who were out of the way. Side by side we see the dignity and majesty of His Godhead and the meekness and lowliness of His manhood—blessedly united and consistently combined into one, like these curtains deftly joined by loops of blue (heavenly grace) and couplings of gold (divine energy).

When the final coupling had been fastened, the women who had made the curtains asked permission to go inside to enjoy their handiwork. They hadn't realized the emotional impact it would produce, for they had worked on it in small sections. When stretched out as a complete ceiling, they realized that the cherubim they had embroidered with the various colors actually touched wing-tip to wing-tip, forming a firmament of feathers upon the ceiling. What protection the priests would feel ministering unto God under such protection of God's mighty angels. Well could the women have understood the Psalmist when he cried: "I will abide in thy tabernacle for ever: I will trust in the covert of thy wings" (Psa. 61:4). Or, "He shall cover thee with his feathers, and under his wings shalt thou trust" (Psa. 91:4). Or still, "Hide me under the shadow of thy wings" (Psa. 17:8).

"Ladies," Aholiab said, "God calls these white linen curtains 'the tabernacle' although we generally use that term for all of the structure. The next curtains, which were spun by you women from black goats' hair, He calls 'the tent.' The inner refers to the abode of Jehovah, the outer to the meeting place for His people. This holy building will be our place of assembly; we will visit it, but God is going to live here. He has chosen to 'tabernacle among us.'

"Now if you'll move along, the workmen can continue putting up the other curtains. You can have a good view of the work from over there where the boards used to be stacked."

As the men began to arrange the spun goats' hair curtains on the ground to be joined together in two sets just as the white linen ceiling had been, they were confused to have an extra curtain.

"No," Aholiab said, "it is not a spare. This time we will have five curtains for the back half and six curtains for the front half so it can hang down and be folded back part way as a protection for the linen doorway."

"Five and six," mused Lael, "why those are the numbers of grace and man, aren't they?"

"Yes they are," replied Moses, who had just stepped inside the tabernacle in time to hear the question. "But there is a far greater reason for having eleven curtains than merely to signify God's grace being coupled to man's need. You will be learning about the laws of the sacrifices from Aaron in the days to come, and you will discover that in all of the feasts God has provided whenever the people are to be collectively represented before God, the goat is the *only* animal used for the sin sacrifice.

"In addition to these five feasts," he continued, "there are six other occasions when the sin offering must be a goat:

(1) When a ruler sins   (Lev. 4:22-23).

(2) If one of the common people sins   (Lev. 4:27-28).

(3) At the consecration of the priesthood   (Lev. 9:2-3).

(4) At the dedication of the altar   (Num. 7:16).

(5) For the sin of ignorance   (Num. 15:24-27).

(6) And at the beginning of each month (Num. 28:11-15).

"It is more than a coincidence that just eleven times God specified a goat as the only acceptable offering for sin and that there are eleven curtains made of spun goats' hair to be divided into two sections of five (the feasts) and six (the six specific demands for a goat sacrifice). These curtains point very directly to the Messiah as the great sin-offering for the iniquities of His people" (2 Cor. 5:21).

All work had stopped lest they miss a word of Moses' explanation. But now that he was silent, they continued to stretch the curtains into place, again joining the loops at the center of the building and joining the two sets with clasps; only this time the clasps are made of brass, or bronze, which always speaks of judgment. There can be no mixing of goats and gold. Sin is judged, not glorified.

Whereas the linen curtains left about a foot of gold boards exposed around the bottom, this "tent" was a little bigger than the "tabernacle" and covered the boards all the way to the ground. Now no gold could be seen outside the holy places.

Since there were still two more sets of curtains to be lifted into place, and they were the heaviest and most awkward to handle, Aholiab sent for more manpower so that they could be finished before sundown.

These two sets were merely designated "the coverings," for their primary purpose was to protect "the tabernacle" and "the tent." Each was made of full animal skins.

The first one was rams' skins dyed red, speaking of Christ, the head of the flock in strength and dignity, manifesting His perfect devotion to the Father by being obedient unto the death of the cross.

The outer cover, placed over the rams' skins, was made of badgers' skins. This is the only covering that could be seen by the eyes of men in the outer court. It speaks of Christ as He appeared before men, for He "made himself of no reputation" (Phil. 2:7).

Arthur W. Pink, in his book *Gleanings in Exodus*, p 225, says: "Born in a manger, brought up in despised Nazareth, working at the carpenter's bench, were examples of what the rough and unsightly badgers' skins foreshadowed."

It seemed that a heartthrob of pride joined rhythmically to the beating of the hammers that were driving pegs into the ground to which this final covering would be anchored, very much as a tent is anchored. All who had helped construct and erect this great tabernacle were emotionally stirred. Men and women alike openly wept at the sight of the veiled glory that was to become the abiding place of God.

But it was not yet ready for God's occupancy. There were still the seven pieces of furniture to be completed, installed, and dedicated; a priesthood to be trained and consecrated; and the tribe of Levi plus Moses and Aaron still had to move their families into position outside the wall that was even now being erected to form the outer court. And this in itself would be a formidable task for this represented over twenty-two thousand men (Num. 3:39).

But the big part—the part that basically benefited God—was complete. The furniture was to effect sufficient change in the priests to enable them to endure God's presence. The largest of these, the bronze altar, had already been built and Bezaleel had merely waited until the tabernacle was completely erected before assembling it. It wouldn't take long to have it ready.

THE BRAZEN ALTAR.

CHAPTER 4

The Brazen Altar

EXODUS 27:1-8

It was one of those blazing summer days, hot even before the sun was fully above the horizon. During the night, the cooler low pressure cell that had been dominating the weather around Sinai for the past week had finally been nudged northward by a ridge of high pressure from the equator, bringing with it tropical heat. Without the umbrella effect of the overhead protective cloud, the temperatures would have soared well past the one hundred twenty degree level, and the sun would have so heated the brass that the workmen would have been unable to handle the large brass covered planks that formed the brazen altar.

Men of the family of the Kohathites, of the tribe of Levi, had already spent several days with Bezaleel learning how to assemble the altar, for they had been selected by God to be in charge of all the furniture of the tabernacle (Num. 3:31). Whenever the camp moved, they were to cover each item with a cloth of blue (heavenly), except this brazen altar, which was to be covered with a scarlet cover (suffering), and then over each piece was to be placed a badgers' skin protective cover. They were responsible for the transportation and repositioning of each item. Since the furniture was relatively small, except for this altar, which was large enough to contain all of the other pieces put together with the possible exception of the laver, their task was not nearly as physically requiring as that of the Merarites who had to disassemble, and then, reassemble, the entire tabernacle structure. But although it was not too formidable a task, it was a responsible one, for the entire system of worship and approach to God rested in the furniture which, in effect, became seven stations of worship.

"That's right," called Elizaphan, son of Uzziel, who was the chief of the Kohathites, "line up the altar even with the gate. It wants to sit exactly square to the compass points. Move those foundation boards about three feet to the left. The altar must be in a direct line from the center of the gate to the mercy seat in the holy of holies."

While they were positioning the altar correctly, other men were already carrying the seven and one-half foot planks that would form the four sides of the altar, for when it was completely assembled, it would be a perfect square: five cubits (by their measure) in each direction. Since five is the number of grace, it speaks of divine grace being equally available to all sectors of the camp (the world). Christ is the propitiation for the sins of the whole world (1 John 2:2). But although the altar was equally available to all points of the compass it was only usable to those who would approach it in faith and obedience. It was not the presence of the altar that put away sin, but the sacrifice on the altar. God's love for, and Christ's availability to the whole world does not, of itself, assure the world's salvation. It is, "Him that cometh to me I will in no wise cast out" (John 6:37).

"I can't get over the sense of strangeness that an altar for fire should be constructed of wood," Elizaphan said to Bezaleel, who was overseeing the assembling process. "I should think that solid brass would have been better."

"Well, first of all," Bezaleel said, "the wood gives form to the altar. It is the same indestructible acacia wood we used in the tabernacle, only there we overlaid it with gold. But no gold (divine glory) can be seen here in the outer court; only silver (redemption) and brass (judgment). Moses tells me that the Messiah must become a man (wood) before He can become our sacrifice. By overlaying these boards with brass, they are able to endure the fire as surely as God's coming sin-bearer shall be able to endure the judgment of God.

"Besides this," he added, "by using wooden boards to form the altar, it can be disassembled and easily moved, and by keeping it hollow, we reduce the weight to be transported. We can always find enough stones to partially fill the altar to anchor it and give it stability."

Because of the extreme temperature that day, the men worked at a slower than usual pace and took frequent breaks. During one such break, a man standing in line awaiting his turn at the waterskin was heard to remark, "If the weather stays like this, we won't need any fire in the altar to sear the flesh of the sacrifice; the heat of the sun will be sufficient."

"That would never do," a companion replied, "for God instructed that a sacrifice must be consumed with the fire that originates in the pillar of fire that hovers over us at night. Anything else is considered 'strange fire.' "

Noticing that several of the Kohathites were trying to fit the metal grate to the top of the altar, Bezaleel told them, "No, it goes in the altar, about midway down. See those hooks? It fastens on them. You see, the fire will not be on the altar but in it, for sin is not on the surface of a man's life, but deep within him so that is where it must be purged by fire. This altar is not built like a fireplace as much as like a barbecue pit. The fire sits midway in its three cubit (four and one-half feet) depth allowing the ashes to drop down for easy removal and making it easier to handle the sacrificial animal."

Aaron, the high priest, had just come over to inspect the altar in time to overhear the conversation. "Since this altar is a type of the cross," he added, "having the fire in the midst of it instead of on it pictures the nature of the sufferings the Messiah will endure. It will not be the suffering that men inflict upon Him during the first three hours of His crucifixion, but the burning of God's judgment deep within Him after He is made to be sin, and the Father turns His face from Him, and His wrath upon Him."

Aaron was as startled as the workmen were at those words, for they had flowed through him prophetically. Even he wasn't too sure what they actually meant.

"The main reason I came by," he said to Bazaleel, "was to see how nearly finished the work was now."

"We're almost completed," Bezaleel answered. "We only have to anchor the horns on the four corners so you will have something secure to tie the carcass to. If it isn't securely bound, it might very well flip off the altar during the muscle spasms that burning produces."

"Moses has suggested," Aaron said, "that due to the tremendous importance of this altar and since it is the only piece of furniture that a nonpriest will ever use, it would be beneficial if we assembled all the men of Levi from the ages of thirty to fifty and explain the purposes and uses of this altar so that they, in turn, can teach it to the people. He chose this age span since that is roughly the ages God has chosen for His priesthood, and these Levites will be assisting us priests at this altar."

"Because of the heat," Bezaleel said, "I would suggest that we gather them either after sunset or at sunrise tomorrow."

"I agree," Aaron said. "Let's plan on meeting tomorrow morning immediately after sunrise."

It is light long before sunrise on the semi-flat wastelands of Sinai, and the Levites were already making their way to the tabernacle before the blazing red ball peeked over the horizon to disappear above the protective cloud of God's presence.

Well over two thousand of them assembled, grateful that the

outer court curtains to the north had not yet been installed so that they could easily spill over into the area the families of Merari would be camping in later this month.

Before leaving the worksite last night, Bezaleel had asked that some spare planks be put over the brazen altar to act as a platform for the speakers to stand on. Moses mounted the platform, using the temporary steps that had been provided, and gestured for silence.

"You all know why we've assembled here this morning," he said. "The largest, most used, and first seen article of furniture is now completed and ready for consecration. Yet, we are not here for consecration, but for education. There is much we need to know about this altar, and much we need to teach to the worshipers in the days to come.

"From the day that God proclaimed His name to me at the burning bush (Exod. 3:14) there has been a progressive unfolding of God and His ways. During the plagues upon Egypt, I came to know the voice of God, and during my last forty days on the mountain with God, I was given a revelation of the character and nature of God (Exod. 34:4-7), and gained great insight into the ways of God (Psa. 103:7). This tabernacle we are constructing is really a scale model of heaven (Heb. 9:23). I was allowed to see the full pattern of heavenly things (Heb. 8:5) and, although I must admit that much of what I was shown seemed shadowy and is difficult to describe, God did tell me that His answer to sin is death but that He is willing to accept the death of the innocent in place of the death of the guilty. He calls it substitutionary atonement. For the present, it will be done through the slaying of animals, but God's full plan of redemption does not hinge upon these sacrifices but upon the death of a redeemer that He himself will provide. He will be known to us as the Messiah, or Christ, which means 'the anointed one.' God himself is going to atone for our sins by sending this Messiah among us and then having Him slain upon a cross as a vicarious sacrifice. Our salvation from sin will come to us as we believe in this promised provision (Acts 4:12).

"This is what God referred to when He spoke the protevangelium of Scripture to the serpent in the garden," Moses continued. " 'I will put enmity between thee and the woman,' God said, 'and between thy seed and her seed; it shall bruise thy head, and thou shalt bruise his heel' (Gen. 3:15). So from the very beginning God has been telling us of one who would break the power of sin for mankind.

"I've already told you," he continued, "that this brazen altar speaks of God's judgment for sin being poured out on a substitute. This altar is the basis for the entire system of worship that God has provided. It is a picture of the substitutionary death that the Messiah will die for the sins of His people. The very size of the altar, when compared to the other items of furniture, indicates its importance, and its placement directly inside the only entrance to the court is further testimony to its significance.

There are at least six very meaningful purposes of the brazen altar," Moses continued. "During the time you brothers have been helping to erect the tabernacle I have been holding special teaching sessions with Aaron and his sons, sharing with them the things God imparted to me about the cross while I was on the mountain. Because it will be a further learning experience for them to tell what they have heard, and because you will always work under them as their assistants, I have asked each of them to take one theme of what they have learned and to share it with you. To close our seminar, I'll talk to you briefly, to show how this altar can be a display of God's holiness and righteousness."

Living, as we do, nearly two thousand years after Christ's death on Calvary, it would be easy for us to doubt that Moses could have known anything about the cross nearly fifteen hundred years before Christ was ever born.

Yet the Psalmist clearly states: "He made known his ways unto Moses, his acts unto the children of Israel" (103:7). And when Jesus was on the earth, He told His disciples: "I am the way . . ."

(John 14:6). Surely, then, God must have revealed something of the coming Christ and His sufferings to Moses, for Christ is God's way!

Furthermore, on the mount of transfiguration, Moses appeared with Elijah to discuss Calvary with Christ (Luke 9:31). As a representative of the law, his presence indicated a prior knowledge of the cross as surely as Elijah's presence proved that the prophets had some understanding of Christ's sacrifice.

Remember that when Aaron and Miriam rebelled at Moses' unilateral leadership insisting that they, too, had prophetic insight, God declared that He did not speak to Moses in dreams and visions but "mouth to mouth, and not in dark speeches" (Num. 12:8). Could God have spoken so openly to Moses showing him the pattern of heavenly things without telling Him of the central core of the entire plan—the Lord Jesus Christ?

It was during this period of time, while Israel was in the wilderness, that Balaam, the prophet, who admitted that he got his revelations in trances (Num. 24:16), gave such a strong prophecy of the coming Messiah that the wise men, merely reading it, were convinced that a king was born in Israel, when the star Balaam spoke of, appeared in the eastern skies (Num. 24:17 and Matt. 2:2).

Those who believe that Israel was saved by the mere slaying of animals overlook Peter's inspired statement in his sermon to the rulers, elders, scribes, priests, and the high priest of Jerusalem when he said: "Neither is there salvation in any other: for there is none other name under heaven given among men, whereby we must be saved" (Acts 4:12). They were not saved by mere obedience to the law but through faith in God's provision, however hazy it may have been in their vision. Paul taught us: "For by grace are ye saved through faith; and that not of yourselves: it is the gift of God: not of works, lest any man should boast" (Eph. 2:8-9). Remember, also, that the thirteenth chapter of Hebrews is not a list of men of obedience but is a list of the heroes of faith.

49

That Israel in general did not seem to understand the typical meaning of the tabernacle and its ordinances is not prima facie evidence that the revelation was never given. Nothing is more difficult to communicate than a vision of the unseen or the unknown. The seer may communicate part of the truth that was imparted to him but the problem compounds itself when the second party tries to share it with a third party. But inadequacy of expression does not prove insufficiency of information.

In the first chapter of his first epistle, Peter addressed this subject. Having spoken of our faith surviving trials (vs. 7) and producing a love for one we have not yet seen (vs. 8) and culminating in the salvation of our soul (vs. 9), he adds: "Of which salvation *the prophets have enquired and searched diligently*, who prophesied of the grace that should come unto you: searching what, or what manner of time *the Spirit of Christ which was in them* did signify, *when it testified beforehand the sufferings of Christ, and the glory that should follow. Unto whom it was revealed*, that not unto themselves, but unto us they did minister the things . . . which things the angels desire to look into" (vss. 10-12, italics mine).

It has been historically consistent to religious revelation that the outward form has been maintained long after the inner force has abated. Often the second generation has already lost sight of the reality while tenaciously clinging to the rituals that originally gave expression to that reality. It is a case where the "how-to-do" is taught long after the "why-to-do" has been forgotten.

That Moses did not know the fullness of the coming of Christ equals our partial knowledge of heaven. That the priests seemed to grasp even less than Moses taught is paralleled every time a pastor preaches. And that God gave such complete ordinances in which the people could get involved evidences the great grace that saves us long before we understand the marvelous plan of salvation, for "If we confess our sins, he is faithful and just to forgive us our sins . . . " (1 John 1:9), whether we understand it or not.

50

Naturally God tries to teach us the plan of salvation just as Moses tried to teach the Levites the ways of God. Watch the wisdom of Moses as he uses Aaron and his sons to do the teaching.

"Are there any procedural questions before we go any further?" Moses asked, his flowing white hair glistening in the morning sun. "If not, here's my brother, Aaron, to talk to you about the altar and worship."

Aaron politely extended a supporting hand to Moses as he descended the temporary steps, and then Aaron climbed onto the planks which spanned the hollow altar. He was nowhere near the imposing figure that his younger brother was. He was shorter than Moses, fatter, and stood with just a hint of a slouch. His gestures hinted of nervousness as he steadied himself atop the brazen altar. He looked over the great sea of faces, cleared his throat of an imaginary obstacle, and began to speak.

"As you will learn today," he said, "there are more purposes for this altar than for any other piece of furniture with which we will be working. It, like the cross of which it speaks, is indeed a multipurposed, many faceted provision to enable sinful men to approach a holy God. Its most obvious purpose is for worship.

"When a Hebrew comes to seek his God," Aaron continued, "he will be aware of great contrasts. Having left the black goats' hair tents of his tribe, he will walk toward the center of the camp. As he nears the tabernacle, he will likely be overwhelmed by the sight of so much pure white linen, with the towering tabernacle showing in the middle of it. The gate he comes through, a beautiful picture of Christ the way, is not only pure linen, but has embroidery work in variegated colors of blue, purple, and scarlet. And when he steps through that gate, he will immediately be confronted by God's provision of a flaming altar. He cannot go any further. This is his initial confrontation with an opportunity to worship by participation. Although he has viewed the cloud and the fire, and has observed the linen fence and the top of the tabernacle, he cannot worship by mere observance; he must get

51

involved. Attempts to worship solely by identification may meet certain needs of the soul, but it is only worship by participation that releases a man's spirit toward God. You see, brothers, God is not to be found in our concepts, but in His conquest—the cross of our coming Messiah.''

Aaron paused briefly to let this sink in before continuing. He hastily glanced over to Moses and was reassured with a nod of approval. For a brief moment his mind flashed back to Pharaoh's court where he had repeatedly spoken for Moses. How terrified he was that first time as he, a slave, found himself surrounded by the pomp and power of Egypt. It was that same encouraging nod of Moses' head that had caused him to continue even though his throat had felt like he had just swallowed a ball of cotton. In retrospect, he figured that it was probably as much the silence that had scared him as anything. It was an ominous silence of incredulity, but the build-up of anger was unmistakable. Aaron shivered a bit as he remembered the cool steel eyes of Pharaoh staring at him as he spoke. Sometimes silence is more threatening than words.

But the silence here this morning was entirely different. This was a silence of respect, of desire to hear every word that was being spoken. Behind it was a rising feeling of gratitude and anticipation. They wanted to know the why of this great altar.

Shifting his weight to his other leg and lifting his head as though looking at the men in the very back row, Aaron continued. "When the penitent comes through that gate with a sacrifice in his hand,'' he said, "and senses that he is shut in with God, his most natural response will be to worship, for worship belongs to the beholder, not the believer. To see God, in any manifestation, is to become a worshiper, and the cross is God's greatest manifestation of himself to mankind.

"Now the *reason* the man comes into the court,'' Aaron kept on, "is for remission of sins, for he enters with guilt and a sacrifice, but the *response* to the altar is worship, and soon his entrance is with thanksgiving and praise (Psa. 100:4). If the reaction to the altar is not worship, then none of the other actions or reactions will be of any value, because the Father is not seeking repenters, doers, or workers; He is seeking worshipers (John 4:23-24). God's goal for man is relationship, interaction, and worship that will bring him into sonship with himself, and the cross is His first provision to effect this. This brazen altar is the beginning point for worship here in the wilderness, for some shall worship Jehovah!''

As Aaron turned to step off the plank, the Levites broke into a round of applause. Ever since the incident of the golden calf, they had been distant in their attitude towards him, half holding him responsible for the sins that came out of that chaos. Although he had always been a fluent and moving speaker, there was a sincerity and a reaching out to God in his voice today that convinced the Levites that his sin hadn't been covered; it had been cleansed.

Aaron turned back to face the men and smiled his appreciation, raising his hands in a gesture that said, ''Give all the glory to Jehovah.'' Then, after they had quieted down, he added, ''Of course the response of worship must be followed by remission. My eldest son, Nadab, is going to explain how the altar provides this remission.''

Father and son embraced each other briefly at the base of the steps before Nadab ascended rapidly and nervously faced the men. He had never done anything like this before, and only Moses' direct order had gotten him this far. His knees felt weak, his stomach was fluttering, and his head began to spin. Then he remembered the brief instruction of his orator father: ''One, take a few deep breaths. Two, choose only one person to look at, and three, remember that you know something they are eager to learn.''

Although it may have seemed like an eternity to him, he actually regained his composure in but a few seconds and began to share with them.

53

"I'm not the practiced speaker that my father is," he began, "but I have learned quite a bit from Moses about the remission purpose of the altar, and I can at least share this with you."

Taking another deep breath and finding a person to look at while he spoke, he continued, "We will need to constantly remind ourselves that the worshiper is invited to come to Christ just as he is; that he can enter Christ sinfully. But he cannot take one more step in his approach to the Father until sin is handled. The eastern gate and the outer court are available to sinful man, but the holy place is available only to one who has had remission of sins. God cannot and will not have communion with a defiled saint, but He can and will cleanse that saint. That is a prime purpose of this altar, for the altar is the only place of remission.

"It is here, at the altar I am standing upon," he persisted, "that sins are to be confessed, that the blood is to be sprinkled, that the innocent will suffer for the guilty, and that the fire will consume sin. There is no other provision for the remission of sin but the cross of the Messiah, and this altar is our type of foreshadowing of that cross. I repeat, this altar (the cross) is the *only* place of remission.

"But God has warned us," he continued, "that the human heart will find it difficult to accept divine remission. We will be prone to 'help-it-out,' to add a little something to it as our wives often do to a proven recipe, thereby causing it to fail. Similarly, men will seek to absolve their guilt with works, gifts, self-inflicted punishment, or religious activity instead of accepting God's provision of a substitute. But it will be faith, not feelings, that gives a man remission for his sins.

"We are aware, aren't we men," he said, "that to remit simply means to pay? It is not a cancellation, it is a payment in full. The Messiah is seen both in this altar and in the sacrifices on it and is not coming to cancel men's debts, but pay them in full. Everything God has declared as the penalty of sin will be extracted by God from Christ. But then, God will not have a further claim against man. The debt will have been paid in full. We must constantly reassure the people that if they have done what God has asked them to do in identifying with a substitute sacrifice and in confessing and transmitting their sins to that sacrifice, that there is absolutely nothing more they can do to get rid of sin. God has to do it for them, and He has done it here at the altar.''

Nadab stood there a few more minutes, mentally reviewing his subject to see if he had omitted anything and, then, satisfied that he had quite fully expressed what he knew about the subject, mumbled a brief ''Thank you, and now my brother, Ithamar, will talk to you.''

The men took advantage of the break between speakers to chat briefly with one another. They were pleased with Nadab's presentation, for he was such a quiet, shy person. It was a very pleasant surprise to see that he could speak to a group. And he certainly had a good grasp of his subject to have stated it in such few words.

Ithamar's voice could hardly be heard above the din of this whispering, so he just stood there, silently awaiting their attention. Sometimes silence is the speaker's best weapon. When they finally quieted down, he won their instant gratitude by saying, ''I know that we generally stand when in the presence of a teacher or a leader, but I'm neither of these, so why don't you sit comfortably on the ground, at least while I'm sharing with you.''

This didn't even require a vote. The men's grunts were noises of appreciation as they lowered themselves to the sandy floor of the outer court.

''We have been told,'' Ithamar began, ''that the altar is for worship and for remission. I want to add that the altar is also for dedication and consecration, for it is only at the altar that we can bring something from secular use and consecrate it to sacred use. It is here that what once was ours can become His. But it must be done by the application of the blood from the sacrifice of the brazen altar.

"This altar itself will be dedicated by putting blood on the four horns," he said. "All of the implements we will use at this altar will be dedicated by blood.

"Since sin did not originate on earth but in heaven," he continued, "the blood of Christ will be used to both purge the heavens and to reconsecrate heaven's altar, just as annually the high priest must take blood from this altar and sprinkle it upon God's throne, the mercy seat, in the holy of holies.

"And we priests," he continued, "will be sanctified to God's service right here before this altar. We will be stripped, washed with water from head to foot, and then the special linen garments that will have already been consecrated will be put on. An animal will be slain to atone for our personal sin, and some of its blood will be put on our right ear lobe, our right thumb, and the big toe of the right foot, signifying that everything that we hear is to be dedicated to God. It speaks of a right to hear from God. While sin will close our ears to God's voice, the blood of cleansing can also be the blood of sanctification setting the ears apart to God's voice.

"The blood is to be applied to the thumb," he said, "because we priests are here to serve the people and to minister unto God. The toe is to be anointed to set aside our walk from our paths to His paths. It seems that the higher the calling in Christ, the more dedicated the walk must be, the more circumspect the life must become. With the sanctified ones, the issue will no longer be 'is it sinful or not,' but 'is it allowed of God or not?'

"In our sanctification," he kept on, "oil follows the blood. The oil is never to be allowed to go anywhere the blood didn't go, for until the blood of Christ has touched a life, the Holy Spirit will not—dare not—come. This is not to say that we must be sinless, but we must be sanctified, consecrated. And, of course, it must always be done by another, for it is something we cannot do for ourselves. We only submit to it; it will be done by our high priest. It will be God separating us unto himself and His service, and us attempting to accomplish it. It will always be done by a fresh anointing of oil (spirit) following a renewed application of the blood of God's lamb."

Ithamar had been speaking rapidly, but suddenly realized that he had nothing more to say, so he stepped off the altar in one big jump.

Following this, Aaron stood up to announce, "It had been our purpose to merely take a lunch break at this point, but because it is so extremely hot today, Moses and I feel it would be wise to break until sundown. During this long intermission, discuss what you have heard one with another, and stir one another's memory."

"Before we break up, Aaron," a voice from the crowd called out, "I have lost my hammer. Would you ask if any of the men may have found it?"

"How would they know your hammer from any other hammer?" Aaron asked.

"I have engraved my mark on its head," he answered.

"You mean you sanctified it for your special use with your peculiar mark? Isn't that just what God does to us with the mark of the blood of His Son and the touch of the Holy Spirit? If any man finds the hammer, please bring it to the altar when you come this evening," Aaron concluded.

For most of the fellows, their lunch was followed by a good long nap, for it is always surprising how exhausting a seminar like this can get. Perhaps it was a combination of straining to hear much of the time, trying to remember so very much, and the heat that wore them out. Nevertheless, they awoke with an eagerness to return for the evening sessions.

It was Eleazar's turn to speak. There had been some impromptu singing and a united praise session before his father, Aaron, beckoned him to the altar-platform.

"The purpose of the altar that I have been assigned to talk about is by far its most obvious one—bloodletting," Eleazar said. "When our brethren come to approach God, they will bring a sacrificial animal. We are instructed to have them place their hands upon the head of the sacrifice and confess their sins. We must help them impute, that is, transfer their guilt to that animal. When we are satisfied that they have given their sin to the substitute, we are to slit the jugular vein of the animal and catch its life, the blood, in a basin. As the worshiper watches this life being spurted out, he is to be made aware that the animal is giving its life for him. It is accepting God's penalty for sin—death—in his place. We then will sprinkle some of that life, the blood, on the penitent and absolve him from his sin.

"I, for one," he continued, "saw this as a revolting, slaughterhouse ceremony far beneath the dignity of the Jehovah who revealed himself on Sinai a few months ago. I visualized myself surrounded by piles of dead carcasses, drawing blowflies, and stinking unbearably. But Moses assured me that God really is not interested in the carcass, the dead body; it is the life He is concerned about. After the life has been poured out, we may take any portion of the carcass we desire as food for that day, and the rest of it is to be returned to the worshiper for his own use, except for the entrails and for the whole burnt offering where the entire animal is consumed by fire.

"What God is teaching here," Eleazar said, "is not so much death, as life poured out. He has said: 'The life of the flesh is in the blood: and I have given it to you upon the altar to make an atonement for your souls' (Lev. 17:11). So actually, then, the purpose of the altar is not to kill animals, but to trade lives."

At this point, Eleazar was aware that new light had dawned upon his audience, and wisely paused awhile. Seizing this opportunity to relieve some emotional tension, the Levites whispered their approval and understanding until it sounded like a babbling brook in the meadow.

Although Eleazar was the smallest of Aaron's sons, he had a powerful voice. He'd have made a great hog caller in America, or yodler in Switzerland. Projecting that voice over the disordered group, he finally got enough silence to continue sharing what God had taught to Moses on the mount.

"We have all observed," he said, "that it is inherent to the human heart to want to give its life to God. Even in Egypt, where they did not know Him, they tried to satisfy this desire with sacrifices, even human sacrifices at times. This desire does not originate with the Hebrew religion; all men are born with it. The religion God is giving us is designed to satisfy the need to give ourselves to God, for God's basic goal in giving us the tabernacle and the priesthood is that we may bring our lives to become identified with Him. He calls us 'His people' (Lev. 26:12), 'His Sons' (Hos. 1:10), 'His kingdom of priests' (Exod. 19:6).

"But I am just like everyone else in the camp," he said. "I have no life to bring. My life has already been condemned to death because of sin. So when I have an overwhelming desire to give myself to God, I have to remember that I am a dead man while I live, because sin has brought the condemnation of death.

"We redeemed our first-born with the silver coin of redemption," he continued, "and it has been used in the construction of this tabernacle. We have brought at least one and one-quarter tons of gold, four and one-quarter tons of silver, four tons of brass, besides precious stones, animal pelts, linen, etc., to build the tabernacle, and in addition to this, God has chosen you men of the tribe of Levi to be substitutes for the first-born from this day forward. Yet for all of this giving, we are not satisfied. It isn't personal enough. It still isn't 'me.' I still haven't given my life to Jehovah! We've all discovered that there really is no lasting satisfaction in giving things to God. After we've given everything we have, we still want to pour our lives out before Him."

Eleazar paused to get a response from his listeners. He had felt the audience identifying deeply with him several times in the past few minutes. The brief silence almost hurt, for it forced the men to rethink what they had just heard—"only the giving of our lives to God can satisfy our craving for Him."

"Amen," one of the elders shouted.

"Yes, amen!" several responded, not so much as an expression of enjoyment; as a statement of agreement.

"This is the purpose of so much blood shedding at the altar," Eleazar continued. "The Messiah shall become one of us and at the cross He will pour out His life before the Father. He will not only satisfy God's justice, cleanse the Father's heaven, and save the Father's sons and daughters; He will also pour His life out before the Father, just as the sacrificial animal will pump its life flow into the basin held by the priest. Moses told me that by faith I can let my whole being get involved in the pouring out as I look forward to the cross.

"I feel so inadequate to communicate this," he said. "My vocabulary is insufficient, and no matter what words I use, they may have a very different meaning to you as you listen. But once the sacrificial system gets into operation, I will have a living demonstration, an object lesson, in which I am a participant, that will help me both in my identifying and in my testifying. As I behold, I will be strengthened to become a poured out one."

With this, Eleazar turned to step down. It had been an emotional speech that was as much personal confession and testimony as it had been a lecture. Because he had been so involved personally, the men were drawn into an involvement both with him and with the truth he had presented to them.

Abihu knew this was going to be tough to follow. Eleazar had really outdone himself this time. Taking plenty of time to get into position, he nervously looked first one way and then the other, shrugged his shoulders, tucked his chin to his chest, and then lifted his face high enough to stare at his father right in the front row. Aaron could hear the sigh of two deep breaths, and then Abihu began to speak.

"We've learned," he said, "that the beginning purpose of the altar is worship. I'm here to tell you that the end purpose of the altar is for burning. Since something of every sacrifice is to be burned, and some of the sacrifices are burned totally, and since we are charged to keep a fire burning perpetually, this is rather self-evident. At the end of each day, we will have a smoking heap of ashes to be cleaned out, carried outside the perimeter of the camp several miles, and buried. What means this smoking mass? It means that some flesh has been destroyed that day.

"Moses has explained to my father and me that the cross of the Christ will deal with a person's flesh life," he continued. "This, of course, does not refer to the physical body or even to the natural life, but to that which is opposed to the spiritual life, the carnal. It is that egotism, that pompous pride, that self-centeredness that lifts the individual up instead of Christ. That is what has to go, and with it will have to go a lot of habits, traits, and training.

"There is so much of the natural that needs to go to the cross," Abihu said. "Since, by identification, as my brother has just explained, there is a pouring out of our life before the Lord, that leaves the part that could not be poured out, the flesh, lifeless and dangerous. This altar is the divine sanitation system, for fire is a great sanitizer, a never-failing disinfectant. This altar is not an educational system, it is a burning process. God doesn't intend to brainwash us, he is trying to barbecue us. The answer to our flesh is not pampering, controlling, or hiding; the answer to all carnality is the fire of God's brazen altar—the cross of Jesus.

"In the natural," he continued, "we glorify our flesh. That portion that cannot be covered, we fix up. We scrub it, curl it, powder it, embellish it, and put jewels on it. But God doesn't want the flesh to be either covered or embellished. He wants it to be burned.

"I'm just beginning to realize that the greatest hindrance to the work of God through my life is my flesh," he said, "and only in the proportion that I will allow my fleshly life to be consumed in the fire will the real life of Christ ever be seen through me; but there is nothing pleasant about the flames. They burn, they consume, they cause odors, and they destroy. I wish there were some other way.

"However," he continued, "I guess that once I really know the altar is for worship as well as for burning, I should always approach the burning as a worshiper. Moses said that when our life is hid with Christ in God, the old shell that once hid that life is going to be burned. He told us that one reason so few people come forth with anything new is that they are not willing to move out of the old. It is like the seed planted in the earth and warmed and moistened until germination starts. Does the seed cry, 'Wait a minute; stop it, you are breaking me, you are ruining me, you are destroying me?' No, of course not. To come forth in the new, the old has to die. The only alternative would be to dig the seed out, dry it, and put a little sign next to it saying, 'This is the seed of God.' If we just leave it in the ground to go through the death process, we won't need a sign, for people will see the plant that life has produced. That's one of the purposes of the cross—to break the hull, to kill the old, in order to release the life principle so we can be restored to the Father's eternal purposes."

It had been short and right to the point. But, after all, a message need not be eternal to be immortal.

Moses stepped up right behind Abihu, put his hand on his shoulder and said, "Thank you, Abihu, for such a straightforward presentation. And now, men, I'll only take a few minutes to share a closing word or two. The priests have taught us that this altar is for worship, for remission, for dedication, for bloodletting, and for burning. I would just remind you that it will be here at the brazen altar that the holiness and righteousness of God will be displayed. He will show His hatred of sin and His justice in punishing it. But He will equally demonstrate His love for the sinner and His plan to restore that sinning man to fellowship with himself.

"Please remember," Moses continued, "that the brazen altar is just inside the outer court and faces the door into the tabernacle itself. Jehovah told me, 'There will I meet with the children of Israel' (Exod. 29:42-43). This will become the meeting place between God and mankind. It is only because of what will be accomplished on the cross, of which this is only a type, that God can be both just and the justifier of everyone that believes in Christ. There is no other ground on which He can bring the sinner into His presence. Anyone among us who rejects this altar automatically shuts himself out forever from the mercy of God. Conversely, however, 'whatsoever toucheth the altar shall be holy' (Exod. 29:37). Only this altar and the golden altar, of all the vessels of the tabernacle, are called by God 'most holy' (Exod. 29:37; 30:10).

"This is as close to a holy God as Israel will be allowed to come," Moses added. "You, however, as priests and ministers unto the Lord will be invited much closer, and annually one of you will be selected to go into the very holy of holies and minister to God's throne. Because you are to be allowed greater access to God, more cleansing, purging, and changing of your lives will be required of you than shall be required of the Hebrew worshiper. After this altar has done its full work in your lives, you will be invited to the laver, which also rests in this open court exposed to natural light and affected by the elements of the weather. While all cleansing and purging will have been done *for* you here at the brazen altar, it will all be done *by* you at the laver.

"But enough of that for now," he said. "It is getting late and you've already heard more than your natural mind can remember. There is still plenty of time before the tabernacle is dedicated to teach you the typical meaning and the practical application of the laver truths. Good night! May God rest you in peace."

And with no more ceremony or explanation, Moses walked off the platform and headed toward his tent, Joshua walking just two paces behind him.

THE LAVER.

CHAPTER 5

The Laver
EXODUS 30:17-21

It was barely past midnight when it arrived. At first it was only a gentle breeze that flapped the tent sides rhythmically; then the strong gusts that signaled the passing of a weather front hit with clouds of dust and swirling sand. The coughing and choking it produced sent parents to the waterskins to dampen cloths to act as dust masks for the children's faces. There was neither panic or undue concern, for dust storms were a common occurrence at this time of the year. What was so uncommon was the rain that began to fall less than an hour after the wind hit. It was not a gentle rain, it was a cloudburst.

At first, the mixture of the dust with the rain produced a gooey mud, but this soon washed off as the rain continued to pour multiplied gallons of water on the camp. The animals loved it and frolicked in the rain much as a bird enjoys bathing in a small garden pool. And then it was all over. But when the sun came up that morning, it shone on a washed camp with cooler, cleaner air and a very refreshed people. Everything had been washed by the water of the rain.

Just as surely as God knew that the entire camp needed to be cleansed and refreshed by the rain, He also knew that His priests would need daily cleansing and repeated refreshing if they were to continue ministering both to the people and unto himself.

So He designed the laver.

Since the Hebrew word, *kiyor,* which we translate as "laver," implies something round, we have generally assumed that the laver was a round bowl on a pedestal. But that is only a presumption, for the Scriptures are silent about the shape, size, and method of construction of the laver. Two things are clearly stated, however. We know that Bezaleel made it, and that it was fashioned entirely of the highly polished brass mirrors donated by that great company of women who volunteered their services in the construction of the tabernacle (Exod. 38:8).

And speaking of this group of dedicated ladies, they reached the construction site ahead of the men following the night's rain to do whatever cleanup might be necessary. They were pleased to find that the badgers' skin coverings had totally protected the fragile white ceiling of the tabernacle, and that not a drop of water had gotten through.

Aaron, the high priest, was pleased to find the women polishing the splattered mud off the laver, which stood about midway between the brazen altar and the door to the tabernacle. His breakfast had been late because his wife had been busy cleaning up behind the storm at his tent.

"Is that you, Miriam?" he said to a woman on her knees polishing the foot of the laver.

"Yes, my brother," she answered, as she quickly stood to greet him.

"I heard that Bezaleel had finished his work on the laver," she continued, "and I was anxious to see it. It's beautiful, isn't it?"

Stepping back a few paces, she could see the door to the tabernacle reflected on one side and the brazen altar clearly mirrored on the other.

"Bezaleel is a real artist in metal work, isn't he?" she said, as much to herself as to Aaron.

"Under the anointing of God," Aaron replied, "he has shown amazing skill. Look at how he has made the entire bowl into a giant concave mirror. It acts as a magnifying glass, especially when filled with water. Here, take a look. Last night's rain nearly filled this basin."

Miriam stepped up to the laver and took a good, long look at her reflected image. Seeing a strand of hair badly out of place, she couldn't resist brushing it into place with her fingers. "It was quite a sacrifice for the women to part with these mirrors," she said. "We never had them when we were slaves, but always longed for them. But when Moses explained how important it would be for the priest to be able to inspect himself before going any closer to the divine presence, and that twice God had told him that the priests must wash at the laver before coming into the holy place, lest they die, the sacrifice of our personal mirrors seemed pretty small (Exod. 30:20-21).

"Aaron," she continued, "you and Moses have talked much in my presence, and I appreciate the many explanations you have given me about this dwelling place of God. I've enjoyed sharing what I've learned with the women who are interested. But I'm confused about the purpose of this laver. Why is it necessary? Aren't the priests cleansed at the brazen altar?"

"There are both similarities and great dissimilarities between these two items of furniture," he explained as they sat down on two overturned basins. "They both have a brass exterior, and that speaks of judgment for sin; they are both in the outer court, and they are both concerned with cleansing. But that is where the parallelism ends. Their contrasts far exceed their comparisons. For instance, the altar is wood overlaid with brass, while the laver is solid brass. The altar is square; the laver is round. The altar has rings for carrying it on staves, but the laver doesn't. God specified coverings for the altar when it was being moved, but none were provided for the laver. Furthermore, the altar is for everyone, while the laver is for the priests only. But the greatest incongruity

67

is that the altar is for fire, while the laver is for water.''

"But," interrupted Miriam, "I still don't understand why there are two places of cleansing for the priests.''

"Okay, sis," Aaron responded. "It will help if you remember that the greatest variance between these two items of furniture is between the agents used for the cleansing. The brazen altar uses blood, and the laver offers water. The blood speaks of the cross, and the water speaks of the living word of God. The blood deals with past sins; the water with present ones. The brazen altar, with its blood, is purging inherent sin, while the laver, with its water, is purifying acquired stain. One deals with our depravity, the other with our defilement. The altar offers provisional cleansing; it answers God's laws. But the laver affords practical cleansing; defilement is removed. While the blood effects our standing or position before God, the water affects our state or condition. Also, the altar is for the rebellious heart, while the laver is for the contaminated walk. And, of course, you couldn't miss the contrast that the ministry of the brazen altar is always done *for* the priest, but the ministry of the laver must be done *by* him.''

"All right," Miriam answered, "I see the difference between the purpose of the two items here in the outer court, but are there also differences between the provisions?''

"Yes," Aaron said, "you could say so in at least two senses. First, as to the ministry, and the second as to access. The blood of the altar makes ministry possible. It sets the priesthood aside unto the service of God. But the laver is provided because of that ministry. The more we priests minister unto the people on God's behalf, the dirtier we will get. We cannot handle the constant sacrifices and remain absolutely clean. The laver is God's provision for cleansing us from the defilement that comes as the by-product of ministering to the people.

"But the second provision of the laver is even more outstanding. The altar gives us access to God's righteousness, but the laver grants access to God's holiness. The first enables us to come out of our sin and into His sinlessness, while the second allows us to be cleansed from our pollution and to come into His presence. Without this provision, we priests would be confined to the outer court forever, but by proper use of this divine provision, we can enter the second court and be close enough to hear God when He speaks.''

At this point, Miriam rose to her feet, picked up the basin she had been sitting on, and walked over toward the laver. Gently replacing the basin on the neat stack, she stepped up to the laver and looked into its bowl for a long time, although it was evident that she really wasn't seeing anything. She was lost in thought. It was overwhelming to think that God was making it so easy for the priest to come near enough to hear Him speak; especially since she had witnessed so closely the price her brother, Moses, had paid to communicate with God.

"If only I weren't a woman," she said, half aloud, "I, too, could be a priest like my brother, Aaron."

She was gently running her fingers around the top rim of the laver and then down both sides as though she were inspecting it by touch.

"The laver wasn't built for our admiration, but for our inspection," Aaron said, as he slowly approached his sister. Sensing a deep wonderment stirring in Miriam, he put his hand on her shoulder and looked very gently into her eyes as she turned to look at him. "The first function of this piece of furniture is to reveal the priest to himself," Aaron said. "He is neither dependent on what others tell him, nor on his concepts about himself. He can come to the laver and see his face just as God will see it when he goes into His presence.

"But even inspection is insufficient," he continued, "especially when defilement is discovered. That's why the basin is filled with water. The dirty priest can take one of these small basins, dip some water out, and wash himself clean. God told Moses to instruct the priests to wash, 'thereat,' not therein (Exod.

30:19). This will prevent polluting the water. The same provision of God that reveals contamination, also offers the means of release from that contamination.

"Still a third function of this laver is for refreshing," Aaron added. "A long day of offering sacrifices here in the desert heat will be exhausting. God commanded us to not only wash our hands and face before entering the holy place, but specifically ordered us to bathe our feet as well. Nothing could be more refreshing. Instead of going into His presence exhausted, we can enter exhilarated because we took time to soak our feet in cold water."

"Oh, how perfect are God's ways," Miriam sighed. Then recalling the song Moses had composed after the crossing of the Red Sea, she began to softly sing:

> Who is like unto thee,
> O LORD, among the gods?
> Who is like thee,
> Glorious in holiness,
> Fearful in praises,
> Doing wonders?
> Who is like unto thee? (Exod. 15:11).

The women who had remained in the outer court after the cleanup had been extremely quiet straining to overhear everything Aaron and Miriam said. But when Miriam began to sing, they couldn't contain themselves any further. After all, just a few months back they had joined Miriam in singing this song with timbrels and with dances (Exod. 15:20). After repeating the verse Miriam had just sung, they sang another verse, this time shaking off their timidity and daring to join hands with Aaron and Miriam as they danced around the laver as though it were a gleaming Maypole.

"Thou in thy mercy," they sang joyously, "hast led forth the people which thou hast redeemed: thou hast guided them in thy strength unto thy holy habitation. Thou shalt bring them in . . . the place, O LORD, which thou hast made for thee to dwell in, in the Sanctuary, O Lord, which thy hands have established" (Exod. 15:13, 17).

For the Christians in the twentieth century, the full meaning of the laver is far clearer than it was when the singing and dancing was going on. They had only the type, we have the antitype, the fulfillment. They had a natural understanding and use for the laver, but we have been given a spiritual understanding and use.

Since everything in the tabernacle is a picture of Jesus, the laver must be also. It pictures Christ available to believer-priests, both for their comparing and for their cleansing. It specifically is a type of Christ as the word of God, which has become a receptacle for the Spirit of God. It is when the Spirit and the word are harmonious that the word comes alive.

Even the Psalmist, by revelation, knew that cleansing could come through God's word. He wrote: "Wherewithal shall a young man cleanse his way? by taking heed thereto according to thy word" (119:9).

Jesus told His disciples: "Now ye are clean through the word which I have spoken unto you" (John 15:3), while Paul admonished the church at Ephesus, "Husbands, love your wives, even as Christ also loved the church, and gave himself for it; that he might sanctify and cleanse it with the washing of water by the word" (Eph. 5:25-26). So God's word, anointed by the presence of the Holy Spirit, becomes a laver for the believer-priest, and that is what the New Testament calls us in at least three places.

As long as we are content to remain in the outer court ministering unto people on God's behalf, we won't have to concern ourselves very much with the lavering action of the word. But the moment we determine to go beyond the brazen altar ministry to get involved with the candlestick ministry, or the table of shewbread, or the golden altar of incense, we must learn to use the laver or we will die when we step through the doorway of the tabernacle.

David realized this when he wrote: "Who shall ascend into the

71

hill of the LORD? or who shall stand in his holy place? He that hath clean hands, and a pure heart . . .'' (Psa. 24:3-4). In the terminology of Exodus, the answer would have been, ''He who has lavered himself thoroughly.''

The first use we must learn to make of the laver of the word is to see ourselves reflected in its message, for we can only inspect ourselves as we are reflected in the word, not as reflected in our concepts. No matter what I may think of myself, good or bad, it is what the word reveals to me about myself that counts. As long as I compare myself with other believer-priests, I may convince myself that I am clean. But when I come to the mirror of the word, I cannot help but see myself as God will see me when I make my entrance into the holy place (Jas. 1:23-25).

The second function of the laver is to cleanse the believer-priest from the defilement of his way and his service. Ministering at the brazen altar always produces uncleanness, because the confessions to which we listen can pollute our lives in turn. But, thank God, the same basin that reveals defilement contains water to release us from the dirt. God's word also removes that sin, if applied correctly. But the application is the secret, for although the word will automatically reveal our defilement, it will not automatically remove it.

Too many of God's believer-priests do not know the difference between the ministry of the blood and the ministry of the water. They tend to return to the cross for cleansing, but God provided a laver to cleanse. They are not clear on the difference between their standing and their state, and once the mirror reveals a defiled state, they return to the cross for a dealing with their standing. But the priest was consecrated to his office at the brazen altar only once. It never had to be repeated. His defilement was handled daily at the laver. Our salvation and dedication to the priesthood of the believer was secured and settled at Calvary. But the daily dirtiness that soils our feet, hands, and face must be cleansed by the action of the word, or we will be disqualified from entering into the holy place and ministering before the Lord.

Of course, the sins of rebellion and disobedience must be cleansed by the blood of the cross, but the filth that daily accumulates on the believer is cleansed by the water of the word.

Jesus beautifully illustrated this when He washed the disciples' feet. When Peter refused and was told communion with Christ was impossible without it, he overreacted and pled for a bath at Christ's hands. Jesus told him, "He that is washed [bathed] needeth not save to wash his feet, but is clean every whit" (John 13:10). Peter didn't need another bath, he only needed to have the dust removed from his feet. And so do we. We need to learn the difference between inner and outer defilement, for the former requires blood, and the latter needs the water. The Book of Hebrews makes the distinction quite clear in saying: "Let us draw near with a true heart in full assurance of faith, having our hearts sprinkled from an evil conscience, and our bodies washed with pure water" (Heb. 10:22). If in doubt as to whether the impurity has its source within or without your life, try cleansing it in the water of the Spirit as found in the word. If water won't remove it, take it to the blood of the cross.

But again we must remind ourselves that the laver does not automatically cleanse us. We can read and reread in God's book and see only our uncleanliness mirrored to us. It is not until we dip some of the water of the Spirit out and apply it to the dirt that it can be dissolved and removed. We need to learn to apply the word to our problems; to stop merely listening to sermons and to start living them. We need to memorize some lavered Scriptures to use when we are separated from our copy of the word. Then when we've heard a filthy story, we can get to the laver for quick cleansing. When anger has welled up, we can go to the word and remove the stain. But you say, "I don't know many Scriptures on anger." Who cares? We are applying the cleansing power of the word, not the reflecting power. Remember what Jesus said? "Now ye are clean through the word which I have spoken unto you" (John

73

15:3). All of God's word has cleansing properties. It is as the word flows through us that cleansing comes.

A pastor who was new in a small backwoods community was very impressed with a little widow woman of the community who earned her living by taking in washings. She was along in years, and her body showed that life had extracted its toll from her, and yet she always appeared to be effervescent and joyful. Every Sunday she made a point of telling the new parson how great his sermon was and how it had helped her personally. Because she was illiterate and unlearned, the pastor accepted her remarks as idle flattery, convinced that she actually couldn't comprehend what he was talking about.

One Monday morning he went to visit her, for she was one of a few he had not yet called on. When his knock on the front door went unanswered, he followed the sound of singing around to the backyard, and found her busily washing clothes on the rocks in the little stream that flowed through her property, and singing joyfully. "Good morning, Hilda," the pastor said to announce his presence.

Somewhat startled, and pleasantly surprised, she rose to her feet and started towards him, all the while wiping her hands on the giant apron she was wearing. "Glory be and bless the Lord," she said. "Pastor, you kan't know how beholding it is to have you bless my home with your presence. Pull up that box and sit a spell. A bit of rest will be good for both of us. Oh, pastor, your sermon Sunday done great things for me. I just kan't thank you enough."

This was the opening the pastor was looking for so he didn't chance losing it. "Hilda," he said, "please be honest with me. What did I preach on yesterday?"

"Well, I don't rightly know," she said.

"What was my text?" he asked.

"Pastor," she said, "I has a awful bad memory."

"Hilda," the pastor continued, "I appreciate your compliments, but I don't think you are being honest with me. You're always telling me that my sermon has done so much for you, and yet you never take notes, you don't understand the Scriptures, and you've just admitted that you can't even remember my text or the subject of my sermon one day after it is preached. I'm convinced that you do not understand my preaching, much less get anything out of it.''

Somewhat surprised, but apparently unhurt by his remarks, she said, "Oh, preacher, you is right on. I doesn't understand your sermons, but they is to me what the soap and water is to these clothes. These here clothes doesn't know nothin' 'bout soap and water, but when they flows through them, it gets all the dirt out and they gets clean. I kan't quote it back, I kan't preach it, and I kan't even remember it the next day, but I can get clean by it.''

Although she could not express it in theological terms, she had learned how to laver herself in God's word. She had learned well the truth of Ephesians 5:26, "That he might sanctify and cleanse it with the washing of water by the word.''

That's how Christ's bride is going to be cleansed. She is not going to be cleansed through the power of exorcism. It will not come through healing ministries. The bride is not going to be cleansed through church unity. She must be cleansed by the word of God.

Now God's word may very well cast out demons, heal the sick, and bring the believers into the unity of the Spirit, but it is the word, not what the word produces, that cleanses the saints.

Happily, the word reveals and releases us from all filthiness of the flesh and spirit. It also refreshes. The weariness that life's drudgery produces and the fatigue of service can be replaced with refreshing as we get our feet into God's word. We don't need to go to church physically exhausted and emotionally spent. A little time spent singing the Scriptures or reading the word will help us recoup our strength and invigorate our spirit. "They that wait upon the LORD shall renew their strength" (Isa. 40:31). How unfair it is to give God our most exhausted time of the day when we have a refreshing laver available for our use before going into His presence.

The first mention of water in the Scriptures, after the creation of man, is when Abraham washed the feet of the strangers that later turned out to be angels en route to Sodom. Abraham told them that if they would allow him to wash their feet, they would be refreshed (Gen. 18:4). Later, these same angels refused to let their feet be washed in Lot's house. They weren't about to be refreshed down there in that place of sin, but they enjoyed being refreshed in Abraham's house.

The word will rest, relax, refresh, and renew us. We need to say it and shout it; memorize it and meditate upon it; read it and recite it; bask in it and bathe in it.

Although the laver primarily had the basic functions of revealing, releasing, and refreshing, to us on this side of Calvary, with the full written word available to us, the laver of the word has at least seven additional uses. The epistles clearly define them.

Very high on this list is the divine energy, which we call faith. "So then faith cometh by hearing, and hearing by the word of God" (Rom. 10:17). The hearing of God's word (and this hearing presupposes a heeding) becomes the channel that faith flows through. God's word becomes the transmission line that links the generator to the motor. It is quite common to hear Christians say: "I have no faith," or, "My faith is a feeble, fruitless thing. I wish I had faith for this, or that, or the other." But wishing never produces faith; the word of God produces faith. When faith is weak, we should return to the laver. Since "without faith it is impossible to please God" (Heb. 11:6), there is no wisdom in continuing to minister unto people in the outer court faithlessly. We need but take a few minutes off from service and get to the laver for a renewal of our faith with which to minister. We don't originate the faith, God does. We only receive it through hearing Him in His word.

A second New Testament use of the laver of God's word is for our defense. "And take the . . . sword of the Spirit, which is the word of God'' (Eph. 6:17). This armor is specifically given that we may ''be able to withstand . . . and to stand'' (Eph. 6:13). This sword of the word of God is a weapon. No man enters into the presence of God without being attacked by the enemy, for Satan's second greatest drive is to prevent God from being worshiped (his greatest desire is to be worshiped himself). He has a thousand fiery darts of accusation and condemnation to hurl at a would-be worshiper. Sometimes we are too slow in wielding the shield of faith and a dart gets into us. We should immediately pull out our knife of the word and remove the dart. No matter what accusation has gotten through, Romans 8:1 will remove it: ''There is therefore now no condemnation.''

It was in his letter to the church at Philippi that Paul introduced a third benefit of the laver of the word when he wrote: ''Holding forth the word of life'' (Phil. 2:16). God's word becomes the very fountain of life itself. Ponce de Leon crossed the Atlantic in a sailboat in search of the fountain of youth, while the Christians had access to it all along. God's word is our life source.

When we are ministering among people in whom death is working, that same process begins to work in us. There is a contagious atmosphere about death, and the outer court is a place of continual death; the stains on the priests are death stains. The only answer to this contagion of death is life, for life is the only antithesis to death.

Furthermore, although our sanctification began at the brazen altar, the cross, it is completed in a daily appropriation at God's laver, ''. . . sanctified by the word of God and prayer'' (1 Tim. 4:5). It is the cross that makes it possible for us to get to the word, but it is the word that effects the necessary changes in us. We should never abandon our beginnings, but we shouldn't abide in them either. To pitch a tent at the foot of the cross and spend the rest of our lives weeping in gratitude is a mistake. But God's goal is for us to become sons and saints. We are to ''grow in grace'' (2 Pet. 3:18); to ''be changed from glory to glory'' (2 Cor. 3:18), and to increase in wisdom and knowledge of God ever pressing on to become mature sons of God. The Old Testament priest had to pass his thirty-third birthday before he could be consecrated to full service. The younger ones merely served the older. We must, "grow up into him in all things" (Eph. 4:15). We need continual trips to the laver-word so that the provision of the cross may become a process in our lives. We have been sanctified (set apart from and unto), we are being sanctified, and we shall be sanctified. The utopian becomes utilitarian by constant application of the contents of the laver.

Still a fifth use of the word is discernment. "For the word of God . . . is a discerner of the thoughts and intents of the heart" (Heb. 4:12). This verse tells us that God's word is so competent a discerner that it divides between the joint and marrow, between the thought and intent, and between soul and spirit. This is a far higher operation of discernment than the gift of "the discerning of spirits," listed in 1 Corinthians 12. The gift enables us to see which spirit force is at work, but the word reveals the depths of our own life to ourself. In Ezekiel 44, which speaks of a massive spiritual temple, the only priests who were allowed to give judgment between right and wrong, and between sacred and secular, were the sons of Zadok, who were specifically instructed to come into the holy place to minister unto God. Having seen the holiness of God, they were qualified to teach what was unholy. Having served in the divine presence, they could quickly discern human pretense. It was a matter of perspective and having a divine point of reference.

Watching football on television, one not uncommonly disagrees with the official's call. Even the announcers occasionally feel that an injustice has been done by the call. But usually when it is replayed from a different viewing angle, we find that the official was right. From our point of view, it seems entirely different than when seen from his perspective.

It is only when we are in the word of God that we gain God's viewpoint of ourselves, others, and circumstances. We must be in His position to see His perspective, and it is the word of God that positions us with Him. Divine discernment is available at the laver of the word.

A sixth additional benefit of the Bible is creative power. "Through faith we understand that the worlds were framed by the word of God" (Heb. 11:3). Genesis tells us: "God said, Let there be . . . and there was. . . ." (1:3). Has God stopped creating? No! What are we if we are not a "a new creation?" We have been born again by the effectual power of God's word. We have been regenerated not by an act of our will but by an action of His word. Satan's word has never been able to undo God's word. Our own words are a puny, ineffectual, mumbling compared to God's word. When we go to the laver, we have access to God's creative word.

Greek scholars have pointed out that when Jesus said, "If ye abide in me, and my words abide in you, ye shall ask what ye will, and it shall be done unto you" (John 15:7), that the final phrase can literally be translated, "if it isn't around, I'll make it for you." When we apply that word to our lives, we are applying creative power.

And this laver is our source of instruction: "All scripture . . . is profitable . . . for instruction . . . that the man of God may be perfect . . . unto all good works" (2 Tim. 3:16-17). Both the Old Testament priest and the New Testament believer-priest need instruction in two fundamentals. On his way into the holy place, he needs to be taught *how to worship*, and on his way out from the holy of holies, he needs to be taught *how to work*.

Some time ago I was praying out of my heart unto the Lord in a Sunday morning service. I prayed, "O Lord, teach me to worship; teach me how to worship." After the service, a member of that congregation, obviously distressed, called me aside and said, "What are you doing praying to the Lord to teach you to worship? You're here to teach us to worship."

I just smiled and said, "I prayed that way because I don't know

79

how to worship as I should. I know more than I used to know, but I don't know enough to get where I want to get in worship.''

Do we really know how to worship? Oh, we know the difference in the style of worship services among the various denominations and can adapt our behavior accordingly, but is that really worship? There may very well be a difference in acceptable response between God attending our services and our coming into heaven's worship service.

The Old Testament priest learned the service of the outer court perfectly. Both the liturgy and the ceremony had been performed so repeatedly that he could do it by rote. But at the laver, he has washed off all residue of this perfunctory service and has been bidden to come into the divine presence. How is he to behave, to function in there?

This is when the instruction of the word becomes so vital. God communicated His instructions orally through Moses to those priests but has committed them to writing for us.

We can go to the book and learn to worship. No man ever excelled Jesus at worship, and most of the New Testament is about Him. Let's worship like Jesus worshiped. Let's learn to worship as Paul and Peter did. Let's go to the Book of Revelation and see how the angels, the elders, and the redeemed saints who were already in God's presence worship God. While God doesn't penalize ignorance, He doesn't reward it either. The laver, the word of God, is our book of etiquette governing our behavior in the holy place.

But Exodus 30:20 commands a washing at the laver before going into the holy place, and then demands a washing again before going back to the brazen altar seeming to insist upon a washing before going in and a washing upon coming out. But why a washing at the laver when coming out of God's presence? There is nothing defiling in there.

Perhaps it was for refreshing before returning to ministry. An hour spent in God's presence can be more exhausting than four hours of physical labor. Our flesh becomes weak when exposed to

God's holiness as hundreds who have been "slain in the Spirit" can attest. While you're in the divine presence, there is no awareness of exhaustion, for we are exhilarated by God's presence. But when we step back into the outer court, and become retuned to our physical senses, we may very well recognize physical exhaustion. What's the answer? Stop by the laver of the word to be reinvigorated.

But the primary purpose was to emphasize that they were back in the presence of the people. And the two ministries are radically different. We don't work in God's presence, and we don't worship people. We get our working orders while in His presence, but the working is done after we have left Him. In His presence we are Marys, sitting at his feet rapturously hanging on every word He speaks. But away from His presence, we are Marthas, energetically doing His bidding.

When we are prostrate at His feet, we think we know and understand everything He is saying. But when we step out and try to implement it, we usually find that we get more inspiration than instruction. We need to go to the Bible to learn how to do what He asks us to do.

So much of the service we render to God falls far below the standards of Scripture. For instance, unless we go to the word, we don't know what we are supposed to love and what we are to hate, so we try to love everyone and everything. Yet Saul was rejected from being king over Israel because he spared the people God had directed him to slay. He would not hate what God hated.

We often get confused as to the type of ministry that should be performed. We owe our brothers and sisters one type of service, but we owe the sinner an entirely different form of service.

Where can we learn the difference? From the Bible. Jesus treated His disciples differently than He treated the multitude.

Although the laver is the only piece of furniture that God declared was to be a statute forever (Exod. 30:21), it is the one piece that we do not hear about after it was dedicated.

Many years later when David excitedly returned the ark to Jerusalem, he ignored the laver, and when Solomon built God that impressive temple that David had designed, he either had the original or reconstructed each of the seven pieces of furniture from the tabernacle, except the laver. He substituted a "molten sea" (1 Kings 7:23) for the laver. Possibly they kept the brazen altar, but forsook the laver because at the brazen altar the cleansing was done *for* them, but at the laver the cleansing had to be done *by* them.

History shows how often this has been repeated. One of the first things to be set aside in every denomination has been the word of God. It is no longer the book of rules; it is replaced with bylaws. It is no longer needed as the source of instruction, for they have written their own text books. It isn't needed as the basis for preaching, for they have current events and politics to talk about. They have limited their ministry to the outer court so that they do not need to be lavered. They have no intention of going into the holy place.

But sad as this is, it is even sadder to see believer-priests ignoring the laver. It is insidious, but we get so involved with other things that there isn't time for the word, so we try to go directly from the brazen altar to the lampstand, from our salvation to the operation of the gifts of the Spirit. But we'll never make it. No laver, no cleansing. No cleansing, no coming into the holy place.

Man's ignoring of the laver does not invalidate it. In Revelation 15:2-3, we see the redeemed saints standing on a sea of glass (heaven's laver) singing the songs of Moses and the Lamb. Without the laver we would never have made it, but the laver fully accomplished its work. We now stand in the midst of heaven's seven spirits of God, of which the tabernacle's lampstand was only a miniature type, with the harps of God in our undefiled hands, our feet on the laver that no longer needs water in it, and our purified faces beholding the beauty of the Lord, and responding in alternating shouts of victory and songs of praise and rejoicing.

Obviously we know this because we have read the last chapter of the book. Aaron and the Levitical priesthood lived in chapter 2, but although they didn't comprehend how it would end, they did understand how it began because they were in the beginning, and even then the laver was crucial in preparing them for ministry in the holy place. They knew that the very next station of worship would be the golden lampstand, which would shed new light on their future ministries.

THE LAMP STAND.

CHAPTER 6

The Lampstand
EXODUS 25:31-40

Anyone who has been involved in the dedication of a new church, especially if it was constructed in part or the whole by the members of the congregation, knows just how hectic the last few weeks can be. Things that were expected to just fall into place don't, and a hundred or more little details have to be attended to. Although the major construction may be complete, minor installations take on major dimensions. Long hours of overtime are needed just to meet the dedication deadline.

It was no different with the tabernacle. Weeks of feverish activity had passed since Miriam and Aaron sat in the outer court and talked about the laver. In the intervening weeks, all of the Levites, Moses, and Aaron had moved their families and tents to their new encampment sites just outside the tabernacle enclosure. The final curtain had been hung completing this fence around the outer court, and the priests' garments had been completed. Just yesterday, Bezaleel finished the final work on the elaborate golden lampstand. It had been his special project, for it was one of the most difficult pieces of tabernacle furniture to make, partially because of the artwork on it, and partially because it was hammered out of one solid piece of gold.

With the tenderness they would have used in carrying a baby, Bezaleel and Aholiab brought the lampstand from the tent where it had been formed to the tabernacle where it would be consecrated to the service of Jehovah. Although he had tried to make the move as inconspicuously as possible, it drew a great crowd of spectators who formed an impromptu parade of admirers praising Bezaleel for his skill and talent. Realizing that this would be the only opportunity for a nonpriest to ever see this beautiful piece of furniture, for once it was positioned in the holy place only the priests could behold it, the two men sat the lampstand upright on the desert sand just outside the eastern gate of the outer court and allowed the people to inspect it. Of course, people being what they are, it wasn't long until word had circulated throughout the camp that there was an ''open house'' for the lampstand. Bezaleel had consented for the people to look, but many had to touch, and the bolder had to question.

''Who carved the wood before it was overlaid with gold?'' one asked.

''There is no wood,'' Bezaleel answered. ''It is solid gold, about one hundred twenty-five pounds.''

''Did Aaron cast it like he did the molten calf?'' asked another.

''No,'' Aholiab answered. ''This work has not seen the fire; it is beaten work. Bezaleel has spent many weeks working with the hammer, stretching, shaping, forming, and engraving this unique lampstand.''

Shelumiel, captain of the tribe of Simeon, who was standing close enough to touch the lampstand, gently fingered the intersecting branches that were paired three to each side of the central stem and remarked, ''He certainly did a beautiful job of soldering these pieces together. I can't feel a seam anywhere.''

''There are no seams to feel,'' Bezaleel said. ''I was not allowed to form the pieces separately and then join them together. God's pattern called for the entire unit to be formed from one piece of gold. When I saw that it could not be carved out of wood and covered with gold, as we did some of the other pieces of furniture in the holy place, I showed Moses how much simpler it would be to make a mold and to cast the gold. But when he rechecked the plans God gave him on the mountain, he said that there could be no shortcuts; I would have to form it with the hammer, and that it couldn't even be made in separate pieces and joined; it had to be formed out of one solid piece of gold.''

Far to the rear of the ever-growing crowd of onlookers came a cry, ''We can't see it. Can you hold it up?''

Before Bezaleel could explain that it was far too heavy to be held aloft for a protracted time, one of the oxcarts that was being used to transport wood to the brazen altar made its exit through the gate en route to the wood lot. Aholiab quickly commandeered it asking the driver to steady the oxen while they used the cart as a temporary platform.

Willing hands quickly raised the lampstand to the floor of the cart and boosted both Bezaleel and Aholiab up alongside it. Raising his voice, Bezaleel began describing his handiwork.

''Basically,'' he said, ''this is a seven-branched candlestick, with a large central shaft that extends higher than the six branches that form the three perfect pairs on either side of the central shaft. The artwork on the shaft and the branches is the same. It depicts the three stages of the almond—the bud, the flower and the ripened fruit. Each branch has three complete sets of these stages making a total of nine, a beautiful manifestation of the fruit of the Spirit that we see so evident in the life of Moses. The central shaft, however, has four sets of buds, flowers, and ripened almonds. Each branch is separated from the other by a pair of these, giving it perfect proportion. This means that we have twelve sets of these stages on the central shaft, speaking of divine government.''

People pushed and jostled one another in their attempt to gain a better viewing position. The shorter ones jumped for a quick glimpse, while others stood on their tiptoes and several fathers boosted their sons onto their shoulders.

"Is there a special significance to the almond tree?" one of the women standing next to the oxen asked.

Bezaleel turned to Aholiab and said, "Would you like to explain that to them?"

"Yes," he answered. "You realize, of course, that we use the same word [*shaqad*] to mean "almond" and "to be alert" or "expecting." But more than that, the almond tree is the very first tree to spring to life after the winter. It is the first to bud, flower, and to bear fruit. It survives the death of winter and comes to life with bud, flower, and fruit before any other tree in the orchard shows life. It is sometimes called the 'awakening tree.' "

As is so often the case with revelation, Aholiab had only a glimpse of the full truth. In just a few years he would see a further revelation of this truth when Aaron's rod budded, blossomed, and brought forth ripe almonds (Num. 17). During the long wanderings in the wilderness after the people had refused to enter the promised land because of the report of giants in the land, many of the Levites and the chief princes of Israel became ambitious for Aaron's high priestly office. After God judged their insurrection by opening the earth and swallowing them alive, the people murmured against Moses and Aaron that they, not God, had destroyed the people. God responded with a plague that killed over fourteen thousand of the people, and then proposed a plan to reestablish divinely appointed leadership. He instructed the head of each tribe to choose a small cutting from a tree, a rod, and to carve his name on it. These rods were then laid before the Lord in the tabernacle overnight. God said that the man he chose would have a blooming rod in the morning.

On the morrow, eleven rods had withered and dried up, but the rod with Aaron's name on it had not only budded, but had blossoms and ripe almonds on it: life, beauty, and fruit simultaneously.

Still many years later, several centuries, actually, there would be an even greater insurrection against God's leadership. A "rod out of the stem of Jesse'' (Isa. 11:1) would be "cut off" (Dan. 9:26) at Calvary and laid before the Lord in the tomb. But on God's morning he would arise full of life, beauty, and ripened fruit and be declared to be "the firstfruits of them that slept" (1 Cor. 15:20).

"Why are there seven lamps, daddy?" one boy asked, leaning down from his perch on his father's shoulder.

"My son wants to know why there are seven lamps," the father called to Bezaleel.

"This lampstand, like everything in the tabernacle, is a type of a coming Messiah who shall redeem His people and reveal God," Bezaleel said. "It reveals Him as the light of God. We know that seven is the number of perfection, and He is a perfect manifestation of our God who is light. Also, light has three primary colors, and our God is a trinity, so we have three lamps on the left side, three lamps on the right side, and a taller central lamp atop the center shaft, giving us three divisions of light. Furthermore, when light goes through a prism and is broken into its rainbow hues, it gives us seven distinct colors visible to the naked eye. It takes all seven of these colors perfectly blended to give us white light. So to fulfill the type of God's perfect light we must have seven lamps arranged in a dimension of threes."

Because so little was known about the work of the Holy Spirit in his time, Bezaleel was unable to give any further explanation about the reason for seven. It was not until John had his vision of heaven on the Isle of Patmos that he saw the "seven lamps of fire burning before the throne, which are the seven Spirits of God" (Rev. 4:5). God's Spirit is manifested in heaven in a seven-fold fashion as the perfect fulfillment of the seven branched candlestick of the tabernacle.

This seven-fold Spirit is seen the first time that titles of the Holy Spirit are given to us in the Scriptures, in Isaiah 11:2: "And the spirit of the LORD shall rest upon him, the spirit of wisdom and understanding, the spirit of counsel and might, the spirit of knowledge and of the fear of the LORD." The very way these titles are given describes the candlestick and shows the relationship between the ministry of Christ and the work of the Holy Spirit. "The spirit of the LORD" is the central shaft, and then His titles are given in three pairs connected by the word "and." In illuminating the ministry of Christ on earth, both through His human body before the resurrection and through His earthly body, the church, after His resurrection, the Holy Spirit sheds differing levels of light.

The three pairs of lamps illustrate the three classifications in the gifts of the Spirit as listed in 1 Corinthians 12. There are gifts that supernaturally enable us to know, gifts that supernaturally enable us to do, and gifts that supernaturally enable us to speak. And corresponding to the three sets of buds, flowers, and almonds on each stem, there are three gifts in each of the classifications. And both the classifications and the gifts correspond directly to this first mention of the titles of the Holy Spirit. The lampstand was all of one piece, so there is always a unity and a uniformity to its work and ministry.

After defining the Holy Spirit as "the spirit of the LORD" (the central shaft) and declaring that He "shall rest upon him," the first pair of titles given by Isaiah is "the spirit of wisdom and understanding." Interestingly enough, the first classification of gifts that are spoken of in Corinthians is concerned with the supernatural ability to know: "A word of wisdom, a word of knowledge, and the discerning of spirits." The first sin was based on Eve's desire to know as God knows. Unfortunately, however, disobedience did not bring her into the wisdom of God, it separated her from God. When the Holy Spirit comes upon the life of a believer, He restores our fellowship with God, renews our access to the tree of life, and then begins to offer us supernatural knowledge, but in limited measure. It is a *word* of wisdom, a *word* of knowledge. What we cannot know by studying or by observing, we can now know by revelation. The believer-priest needs this supernatural knowing to be able to minister unto God in the holy place. Ministry unto God is so different from ministry unto people. Who, but God, can teach it to us? That is why the topmost pair, the highest, most exalted light, is concerned with divine knowing.

But the second pair of titles Isaiah gives to the Holy Spirit are "the spirit of counsel and might," and the second classification of the gifts of the Spirit is power, that is, the gifts of faith, healing, and miracles. The difference between this pair and the first pair is the difference between knowing and doing. It is one thing to know; it is another thing to be able to put that knowledge into operation. Most of us know far more than we are able to do. Most congregations, by pooling their knowledge could write a book, but all of us could pool our knowledge and still be unable to raise the dead. There is in the Holy Spirit not only the supernatural ability to know, but supernatural ability to do. However, the wisdom must come first, for God will not entrust divine power to the uninitiated. How gracious of the heavenly Father to not simply give us the Spirit of knowledge, for to know what needs to be done and to be impotent would be devastating to us. But the same Spirit that reveals, responds! He who shares a word of knowledge also shares a word of faith. The lampstand was not given just to reveal, but to enable.

The third pair of titles listed by Isaiah is "the spirit of knowledge and of the fear of the LORD," and the third classification of gifts of the Spirit is concerned with communication: "Prophecy, interpretation of tongues, and tongues." Prophecy enables us to know what God is thinking, what God is saying, and tongues and interpretation enable us to respond appropriately to God. This is the foundation of true worship. If I cannot hear from God and am unable to speak to Him beyond my halting, faltering mother tongue, my worship tends to become formal, ritualistic, distant, and calloused. But with the anointing of the Holy Spirit comes a "knowledge of the LORD" and a "fear (reverential awe) of the LORD" making worship meaningful.

To go from the seven colors of the spectrum to the nine gifts is not strange if we remember that there are ultraviolet and infrared rays on either side of the visible colors making, in fact, nine divisions. The Holy Spirit enabled Christ to completely manifest the fullness of the Father, both seen and unseen, and the same anointing that rested upon Christ rests upon His church today. All that the Spirit is by nature is available to us by anointing. The Book of Revelation shows the candlestick in the midst of the seven churches as well as before the throne of God (Rev. 1:20; 4:5). He ministers to God and to us.

But the fact that Bezaleel didn't know all of this did not in any wise dampen his enthusiasm for what he did know, nor had it kept the Holy Spirit from anointing him to know and to do the work on this lampstand, although it was certainly well out of his sphere of natural ability. The ministry of the lampstand had actually made possible the making of the lampstand.

While Bezaleel was finishing his answer as to why there were seven lamps, Moses walked over to the cart and asked him, "Is there any trouble here? What is the lampstand doing on the cart?"

"All is well, Moses," he answered. "The people just want to get a good look at the lampstand before we take it into the holy place. I trust this doesn't violate any commandment."

"Of course not," Moses said. "I'm pleased. After all, the beating it took to form it took place outside the holy place, so why shouldn't these who will be restricted from the holy place at least get a glimpse of it?"

Of course Moses was talking of the literal hammering of the talent of gold, but he could just as well have been prophesying how God would hammer on Christ in order to form His glory so as to display the light of heaven and enlighten men's worship.

It was not in the heavens that God did this, but on this earth. It was not even in the courts of religion, but in the everyday world of men. Isaiah tells us that, "He is despised and rejected of men; a man of sorrows, and acquainted with grief . . . he hath borne our griefs, and carried our sorrows: yet we did esteem him stricken,

92

smitten of God, and afflicted. He was wounded . . . he was bruised . . . he was chastised (53:3-5). While Jesus walked with men, they did not see Him as the Christ of God, the Messiah of the prophecies, they saw Him as a man under unusually severe dealings of God. He was being changed from the divine talent of gold into the golden lampstand that could reveal the glories of the Father and light the way into His presence. It was a hammering process. "Though he were a Son, yet learned he obedience by the things which he suffered" (Heb. 5:8).

Jesus was set aside as the lamb slain from the foundation of the world. But His shaping began when He came to earth in a manger through a teen-age girl's body. He began His ministry not in the temple, but at a wedding. He was rejected by His own brothers and sisters, scoffed at by His own countrymen, mocked in His home city—so much that He was unable to do a miracle in His hometown because of their unbelief. But the hammering did not stop there. The elders rose up against Him so that He had to leave town to avoid being thrown over the cliff. And, of course, the devil had his hand in the buffeting. Again and again the enemy came against Him, from the earliest temptations in the wilderness to the hanging on the cross.

Beaten, battered, bruised! Beaten by God, battered by men, and bruised by demons. Why? Because God was angry? No! God's wrath was poured out on the brazen altar (the cross), not the golden lampstand. God was not moving in wrath when He so beat upon the Christ that His form was totally changed; He was skillfully working according to a prearranged plan, the end result of which was to change a chunk of gold into a glistening lampstand. And the work was all done outside the gates of God's habitation. The sound of a hammer is not to be heard in God's presence.

And would God do any less with His church than He did to His Son? If the church is to reveal the way to the Father, then there will be hammerings, smitings, bruisings, and continued pressures applied to her until the divine glory that has been given to the church is systematically transformed from a solid piece of gold into a multibranched lampstand that can form a fitting base for the light of the Holy Spirit to shine out to illuminate the ministries of the holy place. "Beloved, think it not strange concerning the fiery trial which is to try you, as though some strange thing happened unto you: but rejoice, inasmuch as ye are partakers of Christ's sufferings; that, when his glory shall be revealed, ye may be glad also with exceeding joy" (1 Pet. 4:12-13). Being formed into the image of the Son of God may be the church's highest hope, but it is accomplished with a heavy hammer. Religion pours us into a mold, but God beats us into shape. But we need not fear, for God holds the hammer and gold cannot be bruised or destroyed by beating, only stretched and formed. Look at the beautiful job He did on Jesus.

When Moses began to talk to Bezaleel, the crowd gently dispersed. He was dearly loved and respected, but the deep feeling of awe and the memory of the radiant glory upon his face each time he came down from the mountain still made people uncomfortable around him.

It was Aholiab who broke the silence by suggesting that perhaps it was time to take the lampstand on into the holy place.

Moses helped the two of them lift it off the oxcart, and then preceded them, holding back the curtained gate to the outer court. What a beautiful contrast the gold made to the brass (bronze) of the altar and laver.

"We don't need a lampstand out here," Bezaleel said. "There is always plenty of sunshine during the day and firelight in the evenings."

"That's true," Moses answered, "but the ministry of fellowship with God calls for a far more gentle light. There is no harshness in fellowshiping with God. In the holy place, all natural illumination will be excluded. Everything will be done in the light of the lampstand."

As they reached the tabernacle door, Moses folded back the

curtained entrance, and allowed the two men to walk on in. He stepped in briskly behind them, for although he was now well past eighty years of age, he had the vigor of a young man. The men turned left after they entered, and placed the lampstand near the south wall of the holy place, fairly close to the veil that separated it from the holy of holies.

Although the oil was not yet in the lamps, nor the wicks put in place, there was every indication that this lampstand was here to illuminate all the activities of the room. This was a demonstration of Jesus, the light of His believer-priests, not a picture of "Jesus the light of the world," for then the lampstand would have been placed in the outer court. Jesus said, *"As long as I* am in the world, I am the light of the world" (John 9:5, italics mine). But the world would not accept His light because they loved darkness rather than light. They thought they had extinguished that light on Calvary's cross, but God merely moved it into the holy place to forever illuminate the fellowship and worship of the priests and to remain hidden from those who rejected it. The believer-priest is told that he can "walk in the light, as he is in the light, [and] . . . have fellowship one with another" (1 John 1:7). Christ endured all the hammerings of God in order to illuminate our fellowship with God.

In John's Gospel, Christ's ultimate goal is to bring us to the Father. Saving us from sin is only the beginning step. That does not complete the ministry of Christ, it only makes it all the more needed. His work is not completed until He has illuminated every step into the presence of the Father. In His high priestly prayer, Jesus gave the responsibility of caring for "His own" into the hands of the Father, all the while promising them that the Father would send "another Comforter" to abide with them forever. Then He took His place at the right hand of the Father to make intercession for them.

Bezaleel and Aholiab sat down on the floor of the holy place to rest themselves. It was not the weight of the lampstand that had wearied them, but the long, hard hours of the past few weeks trying to get everything completed on schedule. Bezaleel leaned his back on the gold-covered boards that formed the interior walls to the south and the north of the holy place and crossed his legs at the ankles. He was not being disrespectful; he was simply comfortable in this place he had spent so much energy constructing. Aholiab preferred to recline on one elbow while stretching his legs out to full length.

"Well," Bezaleel said to Moses, "what more can you tell us about the purpose of this piece of furniture?"

"First of all," Moses began, "these seven lamps will reveal the beautiful workmanship of the lampstand itself. Remember God said: 'And thou shalt make the seven lamps thereof: and they shall light the lamps thereof, that they may give light over against it' (Exod. 25:37). The spacing and the four different levels of these lamps will fully illuminate the stand that holds the lamps. When the redeemer comes, it will be the special ministry of the Holy Spirit to reveal Him to the saints. He will reveal the perfections of Christ, make clear the beauty to be found in Him, to cause the believer-priests to enjoy the excellencies of Him. When He comes, 'He shall glorify me: for he shall receive of mine, and shall shew it unto you' " (John 16:14).

Moses had slowly walked over to the lampstand while talking and was gently fingering the detailed work of the bud, flower, and ripened almond so often repeated on the branches.

"Few will ever know Him in this beauty of life," he continued. "Most will only know Him as a suffering substitute smitten of God because of their sins. But for those who accept the offer to become priests unto the Most High God, there will be a revelation of Jesus that far supersedes that of a dying lamb. They will see, by the revelation of the Spirit, that Jesus is very God of very God. He is heaven's glory (gold), resplendent with life, opulent with beauty, and abundantly fruitful."

Walking from the south wall to the north wall, Moses stood

behind the table of shewbread.

"The second purpose of the lampstand," he said, "is to illuminate this table and its contents. God specifically said: 'Put the candlestick in the tent of the congregation, over against the table' (Exod. 40:24). The shewbread that will be placed on this table will remain here in the presence of God for seven days, and then it is to become the food for Aaron and his sons who must eat it here. Certainly they could not eat in darkness. What fellowship would that afford them?

"The shewbread is a type of Christ who will startle His disciples by declaring: 'I live by the Father; so he that eateth me, even he shall live by me' (John 6:57). Fellowship that intimate requires a very special light—the light of the Holy Spirit. It could never be done in darkness because nothing God does is done in the dark. Conversely, everything Satan does must be done in the dark, for he is the prince of the darkness of this world. Satan wants a confused mind; God wants an illumined mind. Satan wants a person who is a nonparticipant, an automaton who merely acts, but God wants the mind, will, and spirit of man to live truly in free obedience."

Walking to the center of the room, Moses stepped up alongside the golden altar of incense that was just short of touching the veil. Aholiab reversed his reclining posture so that he could see everything Moses did.

"The lampstand illuminates this piece of furniture, too," Moses said. "God connected the two of them when He commanded: 'And Aaron shall burn thereon sweet incense every morning: when he dresseth the lamps, he shall burn incense upon it' (Exod. 30:7). Without this lampstand, the priests would be unable to see to minister. This altar speaks of worship and supplication—praise and prayer. Praise can be offered without the help of the Holy Spirit, but the high praise of this incense table, praise that ascends into the very presence of God in heaven, must be offered in the light of the Holy Spirit's presence. Holding open the curtain to allow outside light in place of the light of the lampstand would be

97

an abomination to God. Outer court ministries may be done in natural illumination, but all ministries directed unto God himself must be done in the light and under the anointing of the Holy Spirit. God has provided both the lampstand and the oil. To be without the illumination of the Spirit simply means that the priest has either failed to faithfully bring the oil in to replenish the supply, or has neglected to bring the fire in from the brazen altar. Neither is God's fault, so He is not required to accept a substitute light.''

''Couldn't there be a third reason to be without light, or at least to have a greatly diminished light?'' Aholiab asked. ''I mean, God wouldn't have instructed us to make golden tongs and snuffdishes to go with this lampstand if He hadn't anticipated trouble with the wicks.''

''How right you are,'' Moses said. ''The lampstand is Christ, the oil and the fire is the Holy Spirit, but the believer-priests are the wicks. They will be submerged, literally baptized, in the Holy Spirit and set ablaze by His fire. The fire will not go to the oil, but to the wick. But you are right, Aholiab. The wick is always the cause of our trouble. As it burns, it chars and no longer allows the oil to flow to the flame. This introduces impurity. It no longer matters that the lampstand is pure gold, that the oil is pure olive oil, and that the fire is God's fire, for the wick is now impure because it is charred, and, instead of light, it gives off smoke and odor. That is why we have the golden tongs to cut off the charred portion and to lift the wick up into a fresh relationship between the oil and the fire.

''The believer-priest,'' he continued, ''is a participant, not an observer, in the radiation of the light of Christ. The Spirit comes to them, the fire comes upon them, and the oil flows through them. But unless the wick of that humanity is kept in a right relationship between the oil and the fire, there will be far more smell and smoke than light. If pride elevates the wick too high, the flame will not burn correctly; too much smoke. If self-depreciation causes the wick to lower itself too low, it will either extinguish the flame or cause it to burn so impurely that more odor than light is produced.

But smoke, stink, and soot are eliminated when the wick is properly and regularly trimmed and adjusted.

"The more God uses me, gentlemen," Moses continued, "the more He must trim me. Every time His Spirit flows through my flesh to be burned by the fire of God, it chars me, and I need to have that charred portion cut off, for it is the untrimmed individual who has a short-term ministry, and a long-term memory. God's goal for my life is a lifetime ministry, which means I must daily have the charred portion, the residue of yesterday's ministry, removed. You see, the thing that God always cuts is what He just got through using. It is always where the fire has been burning. It is like pruning the vineyard. We know that the wood that bore fruit this season will never bear fruit again, so we cut it off to allow the strength of the vine to go into the fresh growth that produces the new fruit. So God knows that where the fire has touched will never be useful again, so He removes it to expose a fresh wick that can give forth brilliant light. If the goal is to burn, then it doesn't matter whether we get trimmed or not. But if the goal is to radiate His light, it does matter. Our flesh naturally resists the trimming, not so much that it is painful to be cut, but that it is painful to lose anything that was as valuable as that was. But God never cuts anything useful out of our life, only the useless; only that which has brought forth light but which, if allowed to remain, will restrict the producing of further light."

Both Bezaleel and Aholiab got to their feet and stood alongside Moses at the golden altar. Neither spoke for a long time.

"I remember," Bezaleel said, "that in the instructions for the lampstand, it was to shed its light 'before the LORD' (Exod. 40:25). What does that mean, Moses?"

He answered, "This light burning 'before the LORD' is a beacon signal, a guide lamp to bring the believer-priest into God's presence. We can't find God; we have to be led to God. God doesn't need the light of this lampstand, but we do. The same light that will lead us to Christ, and to find fellowship with our brethren, and to worship truly, will also lead us into the presence of God. That is the ultimate purpose of His fruit, His gifts, and His ministry to and through all believer-priests. He first brings the things of God to the believer and then brings the believer to God.''

For some time, the three men stood facing the beautiful white linen veil which separated them from God's compartment only by its thin texture. Each was meditating on the concept of being brought into God's presence, but only Moses actually knew what it would be like. Bezaleel and Aholiab had known great anointings the past few months as they received special knowledge and ability for construction, but they had never been in God's presence as Moses had been. But they earnestly desired to, although they realized that since they were not of the Aaronic priesthood they would never be allowed to come in. Just who were these ''believer-priests'' Moses spoke of as having rights to God's presence? What a privileged people they were.

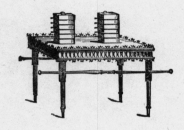

TABLE OF SHEWBREAD.

CHAPTER 7

The Golden Table

EXODUS 25:23-30

As Bezaleel and Aholiab stood facing the veil, Moses knew that both men were thinking how wonderful it would be to go into the presence of God. Only when he sensed that he could enrich their contemplation did he gently put his left hand on Bezaleel's right shoulder and his right hand on Aholiab's left shoulder and, while continuing to look into the veil, said: "Yes, brothers, it is wonderful to be in the presence of the living God. Oh, the first impression may be fear, for He is an awesome God as you well know from having seen His demonstration upon the mountain nine months ago, but He is also a very loving God. After I got over my fear and introspection, I thoroughly enjoyed being in His presence. My two sessions of forty days in the mountain with Him passed as though they were but a day. Time seems to stand still when you are in the presence of the living God.

"Do you remember how overpowering God's voice seemed when He spoke to all Israel from the mountain?" Moses asked.

"If I live to be as old as Methuselah, I'll never forget it," Aholiab answered.

Moses continued, "His way of communicating is vastly different from that when you are actually in His presence. I don't know whether the voice I heard was outside me or within me. But there was no mistaking that it was God, and I seemed to know everything that He was saying as though He were merely reviewing a matter rather than revealing it. All of my inner turmoil and anxiety disappeared; I never had a moment's problem believing anything that God said, for, as God speaks, His faith flows.''

As Moses dropped his hands off the shoulders of his two companions, they turned to look at him.

"I never had the sense of being given orders when God spoke. It was as though the words were far less important than the relationship that existed.''

"And to think,'' Aholiab said, "that this is going to be available to our high priests.''

"Yes,'' Moses answered, "and in a lesser measure to all of the priests. That golden table over there,'' he said, as he gestured towards the table of shewbread, "is going to be the place where God communes with His priests. You'll remember, Bezaleel, that the first item that God commanded me to construct was the ark of the covenant with its covering mercy seat. That is where God dwells in this encampment. It is the only piece of furniture built specifically for Him. You'll also remember that God connected that ark with this table, for after telling us: 'There I will meet with thee, and I will commune with thee from above the mercy seat . . .' He said: 'Thou shalt also make a table of shittim wood' (Exod. 25:22, 23). The ark and the table are exactly the same height—a height that is different from any other piece of furniture. And furthermore, the measurement for their height is a cubit and a half, as though it would require the two of them to make a whole. The ark is His place of residence from which He will communicate with us, but the table is our place of residence where He will commune with us.''

Bezaleel walked from the golden altar to the table of shewbread and idly ran his fingers over the crown that formed a rim around the edge of the table. He walked completely behind it and examined it casually. Then looking up at Moses he said, "I have been jealous of the elders God called up into the mountain with you ever since they came back and told us how they communed with God. They told us that God served them food and drink and that they feasted with Him (Exod. 24:11). How I wish that I had had that opportunity, but I am not an elder in Israel."

Moses walked to the opposite side of the table and firmly laid his hand on Bezaleel's hand. "But didn't you sense this same communion as you were building this tabernacle?"

"Yes, Moses, I certainly did," Bezaleel said. "At first I didn't understand it; I thought perhaps it was the enthusiasm of being chosen of God to head up this project. But when I began to face construction techniques with which I was totally unfamiliar and would just sit quietly looking over the plans, there came a great sense of inner calm, and peace, and with that a knowing as though a voice had spoken to me. I didn't understand it at first, but you helped me to interpret that as being the voice of God's Spirit within me. In a way, I'm sorry that the construction is over with, for I don't want to lose this anointing that I have enjoyed."

"I know what you mean," Moses said, "for I always hated to come down from the mountain, but I have found that His presence came down with me. The gifts and calling of God are irrevocable (Rom. 11:29). The two of you will live your remaining years with the communion of God and the anointing of His Holy Spirit.

"Let me see if I can help you understand what I am saying," Moses continued. "Did you and Aholiab know each other very intimately before you began to work together?"

"No," Bezaleel answered. "I'm from the tribe of Judah, and he's from the tribe of Dan. We really didn't know each other at all until the Lord chose the two of us to work together on this project."

"That's what I thought," Moses said, "but, during these past months, have you sensed a growing closeness between the two of you?"

Aholiab said, "I've never felt closer to anyone in my life." Bezaleel put his arm around Aholiab as he said, "The same goes for me."

Moses smiled. "This is the way it is with God. Once you come into His love and life, a communion begins that will continue. Certainly you two do not expect to break off your friendship just because this commission has been completed, do you?"

"Of course not," both men chorused.

"Well, then, why would you think that God would break off His communion with you just because this specific task is over? The primary purpose for this tabernacle is that God can have communion with man as He once had with Adam in the garden, and with Noah, and with Abraham. This table speaks of that communion."

"How's that?" Bezaleel asked.

"It is exactly the same height as the ark, but it is not the same in its other two dimensions, which means that we will not be able to fully appreciate God until we are in His presence. And, although we may not now be able to comprehend God on this side of the veil, what we are able to comprehend satisfies us."

Gently rapping his knuckles on the top of the table, Moses asked, "What is this made of?"

"You know very well what it's made of, Moses," Bezaleel said. "It's carved wood overlaid with gold."

"And the Lord has taught us," Moses said, "that the wood pictures Christ's humanity. The gold, of course, speaks of heaven's glory. The two materials speak of communion: 'The Word was made flesh, and dwelt among us' " (John 1:14).

In Christ lies our best example of the communion God desires to effect with man. God wants His nature and our redeemed nature to be so blended and interwoven as to create a whole new nature, just as the wood overlaid with gold becomes distinct from either material when used alone.

"Although the table is only one cubit wide (eighteen inches), it is two cubits long (thirty-six inches). So here is another example of pairing. First, the table is paired with the ark. Second, there is the pairing of gold and wood, and now, third, it is two times longer than it is wide.''

"And you might add," Bezaleel said, "that this table top has two crowns around it, so I guess that everything about it speaks of two blended together."

"Yes, and speaking of the crowns," Aholiab said, "what purpose do they serve beyond being beautifully decorative?"

"They keep the shewbread from falling off of the table, especially when it is being transported from one site to another, for the bread must remain on the table at all times. Having two crowns about a hand's span apart affords double security for the loaves," Moses said.

"Tell me about the shrewbread," Bezaleel asked. "I realize that the main purpose of the table is to support this bread and to afford Aaron and his sons a place to eat and drink before the Lord, but I haven't heard about the bread itself."

Moses answered. "The shewbread consists of twelve equal-sized loaves of unleavened bread made of fine flour and baked in the oven. Each sabbath, they are to be placed fresh on the table and sprinkled with frankincense for a memorial, and then the week-old loaves are to be eaten by Aaron and his sons here in the holy place (Lev. 24:5-9). This is as much a picture of the coming Messiah as the passover lamb was in Egypt.

"These twelve cakes," Moses continued, "are to be made of two tenth deals of flour, again speaking of fellowship. This double portion reveals Christ as the delightful food of *both* God and His covenant people. God called it His bread (Lev. 21:21) and also referred to it as the bread of Aaron and his sons (Lev. 24:9). Similarly, Christ is the delight of His God and His covenant people.

"The fine flour of which these twelve cakes are made speaks of the grain undergoing such grinding as to reduce all lumps and refine out all grit and unevenness. Then it can go to the fire for baking. Christ is to know repeated grindings and refinings before He enters the fire of God's judgment on Calvary's cross. But then He will be palatable to all ages and strength to all priests.''

Bezaleel interrupted Moses, ''You keep referring to the twelve cakes, but the word you are using is *calloth* which also means 'pierced.' Which meaning do you intend for us to understand?''

''Both of them,'' Moses answered, ''for there are indeed twelve cakes of equal weight, but they are to be pierced before being baked. They are literally 'the pierced cakes.' Although I do not fully understand it, God said that, before His Son would know the full heat of God's judgment for sin, He would be pierced repeatedly [the crown of thorns, the whip, the nails, and the spear].''

''Do the twelve cakes refer to the twelve tribes?'' Aholiab asked.

''No and yes,'' Moses answered. ''If you are asking me if they are a type of Israel's tribes, the answer is no. When has Israel been ground and purified, or who pierced her tribes, or when was she put into the oven? Or when did the priest eat them? But if you are asking me if these twelve cakes represent the tribes of Israel, I would have to answer a big yes. But representation implies a representative. This shewbread, which literally means 'bread of faces' or 'bread of His presence,' is Christ identifying himself with God's covenant people as their representative. By placing them on the table in two rows of six each, it tells us that all of God's covenant people have an equal standing before God, and an equal nearness to Him. The fact that God ordered this setting of the loaves to be 'an *everlasting* covenant' (Lev. 24:8, italics mine) would signify that Christ represents all of His covenant people before the Father, whether Israelite or not.''

''Please excuse my ignorance,'' Bezaleel said, ''but I don't understand what you mean when you speak of the shewbread lying before the Lord.''

108

"I simply mean that it will remain here on this table for a full seven days. God will be in the next room with only that thin veil separating His presence from these pierced cakes. As you learned from looking at my glowing face each time I came down from the mountain, God's presence is a radiating energy that can be absorbed. That thin veil will no more stop that energy from coming here into the holy place than it will stop the incense of the golden altar from going into the holy of holies. The priests will not be in here long enough to absorb much of it, for it is not fast acting; it takes quite a while to soak it in. But these cakes, which belong to God but represent us, will be exposed to God's presence day and night for a full week. They should get charged with the glory of the presence of God.

"And then on the sabbath," Moses continued, "God calls to His priests: 'come and dine.' Aaron and his sons are invited to eat the bread that has absorbed the presence of God and in so doing, they identify with their representative and commune with their God. They come to the table, the sustainer of fellowship, and feast on the shewbread, which is the substance of their fellowship. Naturally, Christ will be both the sustainer and the substance of the fellowship that believer-priests can have with the Father, for He is the table and the bread of that table."

Bezaleel looked at Aholiab incredulously, but Aholiab couldn't help him. He had heard everything that Moses had said and didn't understand it any more than Bezaleel did.

Centuries later, Christ, of whom the shewbread speaks, said: "Except ye eat the flesh of the Son of man, and drink his blood, ye have no life in you . . . He that eateth my flesh, and drinketh my blood, dwelleth in me, and I in him . . . I live by the Father: so he that eateth me, even he shall live by me" (John 6:53, 56, 57). They interpreted His word as cannibalistic, but Jesus was merely explaining His high priestly ministry to them. Christ is now seated in the presence of God the Father "making intercession for us" (Rom. 8:34), and the Greek word used here literally means, "to meet with.'' Christ meets with the Father in our stead and draws upon the life of God. Then He invites us to feast on Him. Paul asked, ''The cup of blessing which we bless, is it not the communion of the blood of Christ? The bread which we break, is it not the communion of the body of Christ?'' (1 Cor. 10:16). The New Covenant believer-priests are invited to feast with and upon the Lord Jesus Christ as surely as the Old Covenant Aaronic priests were bidden to eat the shewbread of the holy place.

Their symbolism has become our salvation, and their shadows are our substance. What they only knew in part, we now know particularly.

Just as we cannot plant our feet in the garden and draw nutriment from the soil, or soak up sunshine for ninety days as the cornstalk does, so we cannot remain continuously in the presence of God the Father drawing upon His life. But once the corn has matured on the ear, we can eat it and assimilate everything that the corn has absorbed and, similarly, we can feast on Christ Jesus who has remained in the presence of God and assimilate what He has absorbed from the Father. As He lives by the Father's life, we live by His life.

But, of course, none of this was comprehended by Bezaleel and Aholiab. Indeed it is unlikely that even Moses fully comprehended all that this table and its bread foretold. God has a habit of progressively unfolding His truths from one generation to another.

''I'd trade all of my construction ability just to be a part of this priesthood,'' Bezaleel muttered as much to himself as to anyone else.

''Don't feel like that,'' Moses said. ''God chooses whom He wills to do what He wills, and we should never despise His choice.''

''I know that,'' Bezaleel answered, ''and I didn't mean to be disrespectful, but to never have a chance to feast with the Lord is awfully hard for me to take.''

''But you will have a chance,'' Moses said, ''plenty of chances.

Have you forgotten that God has ordained seven feasts to be observed annually? He even made three of these feasts mandatory (Exod. 23:14-16; Deut. 16:16). God wants to dine with you, not just deliver you. He invites you to feast with Him, not fear Him (Rev. 3:20). The fellowship of eating together will satisfy both man and God. That may be why He so connected the ark of the covenant, where He communicates with the priest, with the table where He communes with him. When the high priest goes into God's compartment, it is communication time. But, when God's presence radiates out into the priestly compartment and is absorbed by the priest who eats the shewbread, it is communion time. God has inaugurated communion with all of His covenant people. With the priestly family He fellowships in feasting once a week. With the covenant people who desire it, He feasts seven times a year, and with all of His chosen people, He feasts at least three times annually. All must feast in the appointed place where God has chosen to put His name (Deut. 14:23), and although they will all be times of family and tribal gatherings, they will be feasts unto the Lord. It is His banquet to which you are bidden, and the keynote is fellowship and communion. Each feast is a memorial of life and provision, and each feast reveals something fresh about God and His plan for us.''

"I hadn't heard that before, Moses," Bezaleel said. "I must have been busy with construction work when you shared this with the others. Although I cannot join the priesthood in weekly feasting with God, you can certainly count on me being present for all seven feasts of the Lord.''

"Had you considered that you are actually feasting on the Lord every day that you eat manna?" Moses asked. "This is bread that comes from heaven. It is for all Israel what the shewbread is for the priests. Someday when we have entered into the promised land, the manna will cease, but the shewbread is to be perpetuated throughout all generations until Christ comes to His people'' (John 6:35, 41).

The three men were silent for a long time. Aholiab walked all the way over to the doorway and looked out the opening Moses had formed by folding back a section of the hanging to allow them room to carry the lampstand in and to afford them some illumination for, of course, the lampstand was not yet lit.

Bezaleel had stepped back from the table to lean his back on the planks of the north wall, and was idly drawing lines in the sand of the floor with the toe of his sandal.

Moses took advantage of their silence to examine more closely the two crowns or borders of gold that circled the table top. They were about a hand's-breadth apart. Moses realized that a crown speaks of glory and authority. There was no crown to be seen in the outer court nor was there a crown on the lampstand. Only this table, the golden altar, and the ark of the covenant had crowns on them. Each of these pieces of furniture is connected with our fellowship with God.

In putting a crown on the table, God is saying, in picture language, "I have put a special crown of glory around the place where my believer-priests gather to feast on my presence. Where I am invited to commune with my people will be the place of my glory."

Religion tends to put the crown on its rituals, ceremonies, buildings, programs, organizations, or its sermons, but God crowns the place of communion with His glory (gold). And isn't it when we are feasting on the Lord that we are the most aware of the glory of God?"

But Moses well knew the utilitarian purpose of these two crowns. They were placed here to protect the shewbread; to guarantee that nothing could move it from the face of the Lord. If the table got bumped, the bread could slide no further than the crown. Christ the table maintains the believer before God, and Christ the border secures him there.

While the shewbread is Christ, it is Christ representing us. We are on that table, representatively. What happens to that bread happens to us, and God has attached a glory to securing us in our position before Him.

Inside the crown of gold that formed a raised molding all around the table was a second molding called "a border" (Exod. 25:24-25). The measurement for this border is not used any place else in the tabernacle plans. It is called a handbreadth. All other dimensions are given as cubits or half cubits. If during the time the table was being transported, a Levite should trip or drop his end of the table, the shewbread could only bounce against the blue covering and fall into this "handbreadth" area of the table. How wonderfully did Jesus remind the Father in His high priestly prayer, "neither shall any pluck them out of my hand" (John 10:28).

This word "border" means "an enclosing" and in 2 Samuel 22:46 it is translated, "close places." Haven't we experienced trials, tribulations, Satanic interventions, and eruptions of self-will that bounced us out of position? Did we fall to the floor to be trampled under foot. Did we not rather find ourselves transferred to a "close place" between the two crowns right into the hands of Jesus? We may have a time in "solitary confinement" separated from the other loaves, but we are not cast away from the presence of the Lord.

Moses understood this well. On two separate occasions God's anger was so aroused against Israel that He threatened to destroy them and to begin all over again with Moses' lineage. But Moses reminded God that God's glory was at stake. He told God that the heathen nations would say that He was able to get them out of Egypt, but was unable to get them into the promised land, so He slew them in the wilderness (Num. 14:15-16). Immediately God relented and extended grace and mercy to sinning, stubborn Israel. God's double crown of glory and grace (Eph. 1:6) has been pledged to secure the believer's place in Christ Jesus.

While waiting for either Bezaleel or Aholiab to break the silence, Moses handled the golden dishes, the spoons, and the bowls or goblets, putting them in place on the table. These implements were for the priests' use when eating before the Lord. Their workmanship was exquisite. With the cups and plates set on the table, it looked like a communion table. And so it was.

Seeing the coverings for the table neatly stacked under one corner of the table, Moses unfolded them and spread them over the table and its contents just as the Levites would do before placing the staves through the rings in preparation for carrying the table when following the cloud to a new location.

The first cover he unfolded and gently spread over the golden dishes, spoons, and goblets was a cloth of blue, which tells of Christ the bread from heaven. Only the priestly family would ever see this covering, but it was there to help them appreciate and recognize that the coming Messiah would be above and beyond all that this earth can produce. He would be a product of heaven!

Over this cloth of blue, Moses spread a cloth of scarlet, which is so often an emblem of earthly glory. The dye for this color was obtained by crushing a worm. Interestingly enough, the twenty-second Psalm, the psalm of the cross, quotes Christ as saying "I am a *worm* (the same Hebrew word as "scarlet") and no man" (vs. 6). The earthly glory of Christ was not conferred by man, but crushed out at the cross. We would never be able to see divine glory if we hadn't been allowed to see the glory of the cross.

Over these linen cloths of scarlet and blue, Moses laid the outer covering of badgers' skins. In their ugliness, they picture Christ's humiliation, but in that it kept dust and rain from the contents of the table and afforded sufficient weight as to keep the wind from blowing off the two beautiful coverings, it speaks again of the tremendous protection that Christ affords to His people. With the badgers' skins covering in place, nothing from without could affect the bread on the table. Two crowns and three coverings had secured it and us, thoroughly.

Neither of the men had paid any attention to Moses while he placed the dishes on the table and covered them. They were still so lost in contemplation that thunder wouldn't have distracted them.

Realizing that this would probably be the last time either of them would ever see the holy place they had constructed, Moses walked out without disturbing them. Next week all of this would be consecrated, and from that time on only the priests would dare to enter.

"I guess it is all over for us," Aholiab finally said when he realized that Moses was gone.

"Not really," Bezaleel answered. "Our part is over, but the priest's part is just beginning. Everything we were able to do has been done. From now on everything will be done for us. When Aaron steps up to that golden altar of incense next week to offer prayer and praise to Jehovah, I will be represented in him. I, too, will be worshiping God. And when, on the day of atonement, he goes into the holy of holies, he goes as my representative. What I cannot do, God has provided shall be done for me."

Remembering the chorus from the song of Moses the two of them had sung that night when Moses first told them that God had chosen them to be the builders of the tabernacle, Aholiab walked back to the table, took Bezaleel's right hand, and raising it heavenward began to sing:

> The LORD is my strength and song
> And he is become my salvation:
> He is my God, and I will prepare him an habitation;
> My father's God, and I will exalt him.

THE GOLDEN ALTAR

CHAPTER 8

The Golden Altar

EXODUS 30:1-10

Aaron moved with the erratic shuffle of an exhausted man. The clappers in the tiny golden bells that hung from the hem of his high priestly garment did not give the steady beat of a man walking with a purpose. Although their staccato sounds were soon dampened by the soft cloth pomegranates of blue and purple that hung between each bell, still, to an observing person, it was unmistakably clear that Aaron wasn't his old enthusiastic, energetic self. He was fatigued. He had been through many things since he had joined Moses as his official interpreter before Pharaoh, but nothing had equaled this week. Not even the trauma of the golden calf episode eleven months ago. It all began last Saturday when Moses consecrated him and his sons to the priesthood and with them the Levites. It had been a joyous occasion, as they had been washed, then clothed in their new linen robes, and the blood of the sacrificial animal had been placed on the right earlobe, right thumb, and the right great toe, and then the anointing oil had been placed wherever the blood had touched. Following this dedication service, Aaron had immediately clothed himself in his high priestly garment of gold, blue, purple, and scarlet, and after officiating at the initial sin offering for the people, who by this time

117

totally thronged the outer court, he had taken a basin of blood and a container of oil into the holy place to consecrate all of the items of furniture. When he returned to the outer court to get a live coal from the brazen altar to light the lamps and ignite the incense on the golden altar, the outer court was near bedlam. Everyone wanted to offer his sacrifice at the same time. Fortunately, Moses had consecrated the Levites to help Aaron's sons, but if Aaron had been blessed with twenty sons instead of four, it would not have been sufficient that first day.

Because it was his first time, Aaron was understandably slow in getting the oil in the lamps, the wicks in place, and igniting them with fire from the brazen altar. But just as soon as the lamps were burning brightly, he let down the curtain that closed him off from the outer court, and began to set the golden table with its plates, spoons, and goblets, and to place the twelve cakes of shewbread in two rows of six each, and then sprinkle them with frankincense as God had commanded. Next he turned his attention to the golden altar of incense. He had barely ignited the first stick of incense when God spoke to him from the other side of the veil and said, "Aaron, go to the outer court immediately for your sons have sinned a grievous sin of disobedience."

Before Aaron could get through the doorway, he heard the screams of the people in the outer court followed by ominous silence.

At first Aaron had been unable to see anything because of the throng of people, but when they heard the sound of the golden bells on his robe, they parted and formed a pathway to the scene of the tragedy. Aaron moved as rapidly as his flowing robes would allow him to and came to the charred bodies of his two sons stretched out on the sands about fifteen feet apart, a smoking censer clutched in their hands.

"What happened?" he gasped.

"They were struck by lightning," someone cried (Lev. 10:2).

"Is there any sign of life?" Aaron asked.

118

"None, Aaron," Eleasaph, captain of the tribe of Gad, said as he knelt beside Nadab to feel for a pulse. Crawling on his knees to the body of Abihu, he rolled it over onto its back and laid his ear on the chest to listen for a heartbeat.

"There is no sign of life in either son," he said, looking Aaron squarely in the eyes.

Aaron, dumb with grief, grasped his garment at the neckline in both hands, and started to rip it apart. But by this time, Moses, who had also heard the commotion, was standing by his side, and grabbed his arms while nearly shouting, "Don't do it, Aaron! You are not here as a father, but as the high priest of Israel. You must not weep or mourn for your sons, for God slew them in judgment (Lev. 10:1-3). They were offering sacrifices to the Lord with strange fire," Moses said.

"I didn't know anything about it, Moses," Aaron said. "I was in the holy place, ministering unto the Lord, when God told me that my sons had sinned."

At this point, Gershon, one of the sons of Levi, stepped between Moses and Aaron and placed a consoling hand on Aaron's shoulder as he spoke to Moses.

"The people were so insistent that their sacrifices be offered immediately, that Nadab and Abihu suggested that we have two temporary altars where they could at least take care of the peace offerings," he said. "They left Eleazar and Ithamar with me at the brazen altar and consecrated this area using the censers for altars. It seemed like a good idea at the time. I don't understand why God killed them for it."

Moses sadly shook his head from side to side and said, "God might have allowed them to get by with their substitute altar because their motivations seemed to have been right, but He could not allow them to use any fire except that which burns on the brazen altar. Gershon, you placed the wood on the brazen altar last night, didn't you?"

"Yes I did," he answered.

"And you were standing there with us this morning when God ignited that wood by sending a flame out of the cloud of His presence, weren't you?"

"Oh yes," he answered, "and if I live to the age of Adam, I'll never forget that sight."

"We've been clearly commanded," Moses said, "to keep that fire burning perpetually. During our journey to a new campsite, we are to carry live coals from that altar in a large brass censer, and use them to kindle the fire at the next campsite, for even the lampstand and the incense table are to get their fire from the brazen altar. Everything that is to be offered to God by fire must be offered with His fire, not man's fire. That was their sin; they were offering a substitute fire unto the Lord, and God would not allow it. Indeed He cannot allow it.

"Let this be a lesson to all of you Levites, that while God may bless a supplement, He will always curse a substitute," Moses added.

Aaron nervously stroked his beard as he glanced again at the bodies of Nadab and Abihu. "I can't go on any more today, Moses," Aaron said. "My two oldest sons—smitten by God's hand . . ." and Aaron began to sob.

"Would you so mourn for your sons in front of Israel as to cause the people to feel that God has been unjust, unfair, and harsh?" Moses asked. "Or will you honor the God of Israel who has done justly in pouring out His wrath upon disobedience even if it costs Him half of the priesthood?"

"Yes, Moses," Aaron said, "I understand. Let me just remove their bodies, and I will resume my duties."

"Aaron, grief has clouded your mind," Moses answered. "The Lord said, 'I will be sanctified in them that come near me, and before all the people I will be glorified' (Lev. 10:3). If you touch a dead body, you would be unclean until evening."

Aaron nodded his agreement as Moses instructed Mishael and Elzaphan, who were Aaron's cousins, to carry the two bodies

120

outside the camp for burial (Lev. 10:4-5).

Turning now to Aaron and his two remaining sons, Moses said, "Uncover not your heads, neither rend your clothes; lest ye die, and lest wrath come upon all the people: but let your brethren, the whole house of Israel, bewail the burning which the LORD hath kindled. And ye shall not go out from the door of the tabernacle of the congregation, lest ye die: for the anointing oil of the LORD is upon you" (Lev. 10:6-7).

"Furthermore," Moses said, "since the Levites are not as fully trained as your sons in offering the people's sacrifices, I suggest that you lay aside your high priestly garment, and take over the supervision of the brazen altar ministries for the rest of the week."

As Aaron started towards the tent to change his robes, it was obvious that the people were slinking out of the outer court in utter silence. Climbing quickly upon the pile of wood stacked alongside the brazen altar, Aaron called loudly enough for all to hear, "Wait, sons of Israel. Do not go to your tents in fear. God will not pour judgment upon anyone who comes according to His provision. My sons in their enthusiasm went beyond the word of the Lord, but that should not produce a terror in our hearts, only a great caution. Never again will a priest in Israel try to offer a sacrifice or burn incense to God on an altar of his making or with fire he has kindled. Come back and wait your turn. I and my sons, Eleazar and Ithamar, with the help of the Levites, will continue to serve you until all of your sacrifices have been offered unto the Lord."

All week long, the worshipers jammed the outer court, and those waiting to get in formed long lines outside the walls reaching deep into the tribe of Judah. The busy pace kept Aaron from brooding but it also kept him from functioning as a high priest. Now the initial rush of sacrificers was over, and the Levites better understood the work of the outer court, so this morning as Aaron came into the holy place, he had taken time to put on his high priestly garments, and as he trimmed the wicks of the lamps and replenished the oil supply, he felt like he was collapsing inwardly.

"There is no exhaustion quite like unexpressed sorrow," he muttered to himself. "I have not even allowed myself to show grief in the privacy of my tent, and it has nearly broken my wife's heart. She interprets it as callousness. The pressure of my grief is so great that I fear that if I let down at home, I would lose total control of myself."

"Aaron . . . Aaron!" The voice was coming from the other side of the veil. "Aaron," God said, "today is my sabbath. Call in Eleazar and Ithamar that they may join you in eating the shewbread."

"Oh, God," Aaron said, "I have no appetite to eat. My heart is heavy, my body is exhausted, and my spirit is hot with frustration. Should I eat the bread of the Lord under these circumstances?"

"Aaron," God said, "my strength is made perfect in weakness (2 Cor. 12:9). That bread is my source of strength for you and your sons. I have not asked you to eat because you are worthy, but because you are needy."

Aaron bowed himself before the Lord until his forehead touched the floor. He tried desperately to answer God, but he was so choked up that no words would come out of his lips. Would he always have to learn obedience through suffering, he wondered?

Since God didn't seem to be saying anything further, and since he couldn't say anything to God, Aaron rose to his feet and started for the door to get his sons. But before he could step out, Eleazar stepped in.

"Isn't this the day we are supposed to eat the shewbread?" he asked.

"Yes, son," Aaron answered. "God just reminded me of it. Go get your brother, Ithamar, and join me at the table."

When he returned with his brother, the three of them walked hand in hand from the doorway to the golden table. Their common sorrow at the loss of Nadab and Abihu, and the long hours of working side by side at the brazen altar had brought father and sons closer together than they had ever been before. Sudden death has a

122

way of amplifying an appreciation of the living.

Aaron removed two settings of the golden utensils, putting them under the table, for now they wouldn't be used in this generation of the priesthood. Then he reverently placed a loaf of shewbread on the plate of Eleazar, and did the same for Ithamar and himself, while Eleazar filled three goblets with wine the worshipers had brought for libation offerings.

Lifting the golden cup heavenward, Aaron said, "Oh, God of Israel, who doeth all things well, we thy priests come to thy table to commune with you, and to feast upon you. You have been merciful to us and to your people, and we bless your holy name."

Touching the rim of his goblet to those held in the hands of his sons, as though making a toast, the three of them poured out the wine on the dirt floor in unison before the Lord, for this was His portion of the feast.

Using the golden spoons, each of the men began to eat the shewbread. They found it to be a pleasant change from the manna, and not the least bit stale, although it had been exposed on the table for over a week.

Although the meal had started in awed silence, it was not long until the three of them were conversing most amiably, and then quite animatedly. It was as though a great burden had rolled off their shoulders and they were relaxing after a hard day of labor. Aaron began to sense a song deep within his spirit, and Eleazar heard himself laughing out loud at something Ithamar said.

"I'm glad we poured that wine out on the floor," he said, "or I would think we were both drunk, dad."

"Quite right, my son," Aaron said, "but I have never found a wine that could gladden man's heart so quickly or give such genuine inner peace. Surely this 'bread of His presence' gives the life of God to His priests. We have survived the first week of our ministry without the benefit of this life; this next week should be much easier for us."

The men ate heartily, for the meal that had been prepared for five

123

now had to be consumed by three. By the time they had finished, all three men were in a jovial and contented mood, and felt the joy and enthusiasm for their tasks that they had experienced before God's judgment had fallen on the other two sons of Aaron.

"Dad," Ithamar said, "I have stayed in the outer court all week long because we were so shorthanded, but we three are the only remaining priests who have the right to minister in here before the Lord. I need to learn how to trim the lamps, set this table, and burn the incense. Wouldn't this be as good a time as any to show both of us?"

"All right, we can start by putting out the shewbread," Aaron answered. "The fresh cakes are on a golden plate under the blue cloth over there. Mother helped me to prepare them last night."

After the golden table had been set to Aaron's satisfaction, the three of them walked over to the golden altar of incense, which was the smallest piece of furniture in the tabernacle, measuring only one cubit square, and standing two cubits high.

"Before God described this altar or even gave us the materials with which to construct it, He told us what it was to be used for," Aaron said. " 'Thou shalt make an altar to burn incense upon' (Exod. 30:1) were His exact words. The altar is the highest plane of worship we can come to before going on into the presence of God. It speaks of prayer, intercession, praise, and worship as performed by the priest on behalf of God."

"Why is it so much smaller than the brazen altar if this altar is for ministering unto God?" Eleazar asked.

"Well," Aaron answered, "it may be for a variety of reasons, the most obvious of which is that the brazen altar meets man's need of deliverance from sin, while this golden altar provides man a way to worship. It is the difference between receiving from Him and giving unto Him, and the former is always far more sought after than the latter. A second reason for the extreme difference in size is that the brazen altar is available to the whosoever, while the golden altar is available only to the priests.

124

"But the least obvious, and yet perhaps the most important reason, is what the two altars speak of," Aaron continued. "It was you two, with Nadab and Abihu, who lectured all of the Levites on the purposes of the brazen altar. You taught them that it speaks of the coming Christ being God's sacrifice for sin, and our substitute to take God's wrath. That altar secures our justification. This altar is concerned with worship. It assures our access to God's presence. Whereas the altar in the outer court pictures a dying sacrifice, the altar in the holy place typifies a living intercessor (Heb. 7:25). Perhaps it is singular in its dimension to show that there is only one object of our prayers, praises, and worship, the Lord our God."

"What significance does the two cubits height have?" Ithamar asked.

"Perhaps this signifies," Aaron explained, "that the worship by us here on earth is inseparably connected with the worship in heaven."

It seems a shame that Aaron had to say "perhaps," but he was the first priest, and he had limited knowledge.

As the revelation of worship has unfolded through the Scriptures, much more attestation to this truth has been given. Paul wrote: ". . . I fall down on my knees and pray to the Father of all the great family of God—some of them already in heaven and some down here on earth—(Eph. 3:14-15, LB) while John, the beloved, wrote: "And when he had taken the book, the four beasts and four and twenty elders fell down before the Lamb, having every one of them harps, and golden vials full of odours [or incense], which are the prayers of saints" (Rev. 5:8). While the songwriter may want us to sing, "we are not divided, all one body we . . ." the Bible clearly teaches that the living church is indeed divided between heaven and earth. Death does not incapacitate a believer-priest from worshiping—it only transfers him from earth's altar of incense where we know in part to heaven's golden altar, where we shall know fully. The worship of the saints on earth gets mingled with the worship in heaven through the ministry of

125

the burning incense. In John's great vision into the heavenlies, he saw this most conclusively: "And another angel came and stood at the altar, having a golden censer; and there was given unto him much incense, that he should offer it with the prayers of all saints upon the golden altar which was before the throne. And the smoke of the incense, which came with the prayers of the saints, ascended up before God out of the angel's hand" (Rev. 8:3-4). As our worship ascends into heaven, this angel mixes heaven's worship (incense) with it so that by the time it gets to the nostrils of God, it is acceptable. All odors of flesh and soul are overridden with the pure fragrance of the worship of heaven's redeemed saints and the holy angels. Hence, the golden altar of incense stood two cubits high as it reached upward from the earth.

Aaron and his sons were aware that this golden altar was not solid gold, as the lampstand, but was wood overlaid with gold. Four of the seven pieces of furniture were constructed of this acacia wood, which speaks of the incorruptible humanity of our Lord Jesus Christ. The ark, which contained God's covenant, this altar of incense, which provided intercession and worship, and the table of shewbread, which offered fellowship, were acacia wood overlaid with gold while the brazen altar was wood overlaid with brass or bronze. The ark speaks of His incarnation; the altar of incense exhibits His walk with God, the table of shewbread unveiled Him as God's representative on earth, while the brazen altar manifests Him as God's sacrificial Lamb.

But none of these pieces bared one square inch of wood for the human eye to see. Christ's humanity gave form and substance to His ministry, but was beautifully concealed under gold (divine glory) on the first three, and brass (judgment) on the outer court piece of furniture. This blending of heaven and earth demonstrates four separate relationships Christ offers to His covenant people. As the gold covered ark of the covenant, He is the head of the church which has become His body on earth. As the golden altar, He is their intercessor before the Father day and night. As the golden table, He has become their representative in the Father's presence, and as the brass altar, He is their substitute who accepted God's wrath for them.

The wood and gold though expertly bonded revealed the unique God-man, perfectly uniting God and man. As surely as the vegetable and mineral kingdoms were united in these items, so earth and heaven are blended in the person and the work of Christ Jesus.

Aaron gently ran his finger around the top of the golden crown that circled the eighteen-inch-square altar top. ''The three pieces of furniture that are made of wood and overlaid with gold all have a crown around their top,'' he said. ''The crown on the table is the crown of a prophet who gets man and God back into fellowship through communication, while the crown here on the altar is the crown of a priest who alone can make intercession for the people. The crown on the ark of the covenant is the crown of a king who is both the law-giver, and the law-protector. Happily, our coming Messiah will wear all three crowns as our prophet, priest, and king. He will be the revealer of God to men; the responder unto God for men, and the ruler with God over men.''

Eleazar gestured somewhat idly with a slow motion of his hand over the burning incense, and then put the palm of his hand to his nose to capture a close smell of the fragrance of the burning incense.

''Ummm,'' he sighed, ''it is such a sweet aroma, and yet extremely pleasant. What does it have in it, father?''

''There are four sweet spices combined to form this incense, son,'' Aaron answered. ''Stacte, onycha, and galbanum are equally mixed to form one-half of the composition, and pure frankincense forms the other half (Exod. 30:34). These gums and spices are broken from the trees, beaten very fine, blended after the art of the apothecary, bound together, and then burned here on this altar. God specifically told Moses that this incense was to be sweet, pure, and most holy, for it speaks of the preciousness of Christ's

127

intercessions and praises before God. Most certainly, these are sweet to God's nostrils, and, unlike our praise, contain nothing to defile His worship—it is ultimately pure. While our ministry here at the altar is holy, Christ's ministry is 'most holy.' Ours is the administration of a ritual, but His is the accomplishment of a reality.''

''You are speaking in the present tense now,'' Ithamar pointed out. ''Before you have always spoken of the ministries of the Messiah in the future tense.''

''Yes, I know,'' Aaron said. ''Most of the appointments of this tabernacle speak of things to come. But God told Moses that this was to be a 'perpetual incense' (Exod. 30:8). It depicts a ministry that has been going on since before the creation of man, and will continue long after the saints of God have been gathered into heaven. Worship is, always has been, and always will be the main activity of heaven's inhabitants. Therefore, worship is the highest state a believer-priest can reach while still here on the earth. As surely as this golden altar is the final piece of furniture we minister at before entering into the presence of God in the holy of holies, so worship is the final, highest, and transitional act of a believer-priest before entering into the holy presence of his divine God, and it will be the first act he performs when he is ushered into God's presence, just as we will always take a censer of incense into the holy place with us as we enter.''

That this altar of incense speaks of prayer is unmistakably clear to us New Testament saints. David wrote: ''Let my prayer be set forth before thee as incense . . .'' (Psa. 141:2) and John spoke of the twenty-four elders ''having every one of them . . . golden vials full of [incense], which are the prayers of the saints'' (Rev. 5:8). But this is not prayer that is concerned with people, but with God. It is not so much petition as it is praise. Its purpose is not to beg, but to bless; not to entreat, but to exalt the one seated on heaven's throne. The needs of people are cared for in the outer courts; the needs of God are ministered unto at this altar.

Naturally this prayer of adoration is the highest order of prayer. It is intercession whereby Christ Jesus, our high priest, takes our place in pleading before the Father, not for our justification, which has been secured at His cross, but for our maintenance in the place of fullest acceptance before God as a sweet savor. The wondrous efficacy of our high priest's intercession is illustrated in God's provision of grace at the sin of Korah and his company (Num. 16), when they repudiated Aaron as their high priest. After God judged Korah, He sent a plague upon the people as punishment for following Korah. Aaron, the high priest, was told to "take a censer, and put fire therein from off the altar, and put on incense, and go quickly unto the congregation, and make an atonement for them. And he stood between the dead and the living; and the plague was stayed (Num. 16:46, 48).

God's great displeasure with our self-centeredness, our pride, and our perpetual "improvements" upon His ways is appeased by Christ's intercessory incense, and we are retained as His covenant people. His intercession is not so much an asking as it is an acclaiming. It is not a pleading, but a proclaiming of God's provision.

How all believer-priests need to learn this kind of prayer. We need not get involved with the problems, but with the promises. We do not pray to overcome God's reluctance, but to come over to God's abundance. We must not plead our privation, but His provision, for it is not the desperateness of our need, but the definiteness of His word that invokes our intercession.

But less obvious is the truth that this golden altar is equally a place of praise and worship. Christ is quoted as saying: "In the midst of the church will I sing praise unto thee" (Heb. 2:12). Accordingly, we are admonished, *"by Him* therefore let us offer the sacrifice of praise to God continually" (Heb. 13:15, italics mine). We need the mediation of Christ as much for getting our praises into the presence of God as we do to get our prayers before Him. He praises for, with, and in the midst of the believer-priest, but His praises are always assured of getting through to the Father.

By Christ Jesus the church is enabled to worship, not merely work, for He makes our worship available and acceptable unto God. The worship at this altar is concerned with the person and the wants of God, not man, and is expressed in prayer, intercession, praise, and adoration. It pours forth to God but affects man. Just as the incense does, all worship goes through the single thickness veil into the presence of God, but also saturates the robes of the priests so that the worshiper and the worshiped smell alike; each is the beneficiary.

While the desire to worship may be inherent to our nature, the ability to worship God is only innate in our new nature. Before Christ we had the want to worship, but since Christ we have the way of worship. Peter said, ''Ye also, as lively stones, are built up a spiritual house, an holy priesthood, to offer up spiritual sacrifices, acceptable to God by Jesus Christ'' (1 Peter 2:5). So it is Christ, the interceding and worshiping high priest, who makes all worship acceptable unto God. All incense (worship) must be burned on the golden altar (Christ Jesus) if it is ever to come into God's presence, for only this altar is positioned just in front of the veil only a few feet from the mercy seat of God.

Although Aaron and his sons did not understand these things fully as we do because of the enlarged revelation, they did know that they were only a type of something far better which was to come.

Stepping behind the altar so as to reach the reserve supply, Aaron handed a stick of this special incense to each of his sons.

''Get used to it,'' he said. ''Be able to identify its fragrance even in your sleep. We three are the only ones in all of Israel who will be allowed to handle it. And since God has commanded the death penalty for every other person who makes and uses this fragrance (Exod. 30:38), we must be alert in smelling every worshiper who comes to the brazen altar. God will not allow any counterfeiting of the fragrance of His presence, nor will He allow the sweet fragrance of worship to be put on human flesh. This incense is His and His alone."

"But how will they know the fragrance of divine worship since they are not allowed to enter the holy place?" Ithamar asked.

"They can smell the fragrance on us," Aaron said. "Our hair, skin, and robes will be saturated with the incense. Everyone who comes to the brazen altar should get a good sample of the fragrance of the golden altar from us. Worshipers always bring the fragrance of God to the penitent."

"I well remember the strong prohibitions God gave to Moses as to what can and what cannot be offered unto God here," Eleazar said.

"So do I," Ithamar said. "There were four things Moses emphasized (Exod. 30:9). First, we cannot offer any strange incense here."

"It is either God's provision of worship or none at all," Eleazar chimed in.

"God gives us the true, and He has a right to reject the false," Aaron said.

"Second," Ithamar continued, "God prohibited any burnt sacrifice being offered here. Third, He banned all meal offerings from being burned here, and fourth, He refused to allow the drink offerings to be poured out on this altar."

Putting his hands on their shoulders, Aaron said, "I'm proud that you remembered these injunctions, but do you understand them?"

"I sure don't," Eleazar said.

"Neither do I," Ithamar admitted.

"It is really quite simple," Aaron said. "God doesn't want us to get the two altars confused. The brazen altar in the outer court is given to handle sin. It is concerned with sacrifice and salvation. It is oriented to man's needs. But this golden altar here in the holy place has been given to handle worship. In here we are not to be concerned with our sins and Christ's sacrifice for them. That was settled at the other altar. Here we are concerned with the person of Christ, not His work. Here we contemplate Him as seated at the right hand of the Father, making intercession for us, not as the suffering bleeding Lamb of God hanging on a cross. To bring anything from the brazen altar to this golden altar would be to defile it except for the annual application of blood that is to be applied to every piece of furniture.''

"Well, then, that blood ties the two altars together, doesn't it?'' Ithamar asked.

"Yes, of course,'' Aaron said. "But they are tied together far more by common fire than by the annual sprinkling of blood.''

"And that fire also ties this altar to the lampstand, doesn't it?''Eleazar said.

"Right, son,'' Aaron answered. "God commanded us to burn incense every morning when we come in to tend the lamps and in the evenings when we tend them again. We can only come to the ark of the covenant once a year, and we come to the table once a week, but we tend this golden altar at least twice daily. Every time we tend the lamps, we are to add more incense to the fire.''

Isn't it true that our worship is always in proportion to the manifestation of the Spirit? Without the light of the Spirit, our worship is confused. True worship is done while the Spirit is being manifest. As Arthur W. Pink puts it: "Every fresh kindling or exercise of the spirit in our hearts, results in new outbursts of praise unto God: all worship is ever in proportion to the manifestation of the Spirit's power'' (p. 288). The lampstand and the altar of incense are inseparably linked together.

But then so are the incense and the holy of holies connected. No incense, no entrance. That's why Aaron spent so much time teaching his sons how to minister here at the altar of incense, for the next station of worship was the ark of the covenant with its mercy seat lid. There they would stand face to face with God, and it would be the worship that would enable them to endure the experience.

THE ARK OF THE COVENANT.

CHAPTER 9

The Ark

EXODUS 25:10-16

As each of the three men finished fingering and smelling the incense he put it on the altar next to a live coal, and watched as swirling smoke ascended up towards the white curtained ceiling.

Stepping back away from the table they observed that some of the incense smoke was filtering through the beautifully decorated veil that separated the two compartments. Of all of the splendors of this holy place the veil truly excelled them all. The outstretched wings of the cherubim embroidered on it gave a sense of sentries standing on guard. Although it was only a thin linen curtain richly ornamented it might as well have been electronically controlled steel doors, for once the tabernacle was set up no one was going to walk through that veil into God's sanctuary. No one, that is, except Moses when God signaled him to enter, and the high priest on the day of atonement.

Throughout Israel's generations going through the veil was viewed as tantamount to suicide. Historians have recorded that the high priest used to tie a long rope onto one ankle leaving the other end outside of the tabernacle so that his body could be recovered in the event God slew him.

"Oh I hope I never have to go through that veil to stand in God's presence," Eleazar said. "It is awesome enough just to stand here and look towards the ark."

Aaron looked sympathetically into his son's eyes and then said, "I know, my son; believe me, I know! While I live it will be my responsibility to enter but some day it will be yours. Nonetheless, God has done everything possible to make entering into His presence easy and fearless. He has clearly stated who has permission to enter, what they must do before entering, when they may come in, and what they may expect once they have passed through the veil."

"I understand that first provision," Ithamar said, "for only the high priest may enter the holy of holies so that limits it to our lineage, doesn't it?"

"Yes," Aaron answered, "with one exception."

"I didn't know there were any exceptions," Ithamar responded.

"Whenever God wants to communicate with Moses the cloud that hovers over the tabernacle will descend into the holy of holies and Moses is to go on in to receive directions from God who will speak from the mercy seat."

"Does he have to make all of the preparations that we have been commanded to make before entering?" Eleazar asked.

"No," Aaron answered. "When the cloud dips low he has been instructed to go directly into the presence of God."

"That's certainly not true of us, is it?" Ithamar asked. "We have to be stripped in the outer court and washed with fresh water. Then we are robed in the special white priestly garments, and anointed with both blood and oil."

"That's just what is done for us by another," Eleazar added. "After they are through we begin. We have to offer a special sacrifice for sin at the brazen altar, stop and wash at the laver, enter and trim the wicks of the lampstand, minister at the table of shewbread, and then get a basin of blood, and fill a golden censer with fire and incense. It will take us the better part of the morning just to get ready to go in."

136

"But remember," Aaron added, "that we only go in once a year on the Day of Atonement. Moses may be called in to God's presence several times a month. Besides, God did a thorough purging work in Moses on the mountain before giving him the law. He is perpetually ready to stand before God. He doesn't need ceremonial cleansings, he has been celestially cleansed."

"But even after we have done everything God has instructed us to do it won't be easy to enter, will it?" Eleazar asked.

"The difficulty will lie entirely in our fear levels," Aaron answered, "and God has done much to reduce these levels."

"Like what?" Ithamar asked.

"Well," Aaron answered, "for one thing He lets us bring in something with which we are very familiar. In one hand is a basin of blood, and in the other is a censer of incense. These are items we use all year long. Carrying them into God's compartment not only ties the work of the whole year to the work on this special day but it will act as a security blanket, plus it will give us something to do with our hands."

"Yes, that will help me for sure," Ithamar said. "I never know what to do with my hands."

"Is that why you've been tying and untying knots in the sash of your robe?" Eleazar teased. "You'll wear out two sashes for every robe you own."

"After all we've been through this week I'm surprised that he's not tying knots in our sashes too," Aaron remarked. "But I will admit that your knot tying would be a bit out of place in God's presence."

Smiling at Eleazar, Aaron playfully gave Ithamar a push on the head as all three of them chuckled.

"Always remember," Aaron continued, "that God has sought to make us comfortable in His presence. He even designed His compartment to be exactly like ours so we wouldn't feel out of place in there. The only difference is the furniture. God's furniture . . ." but the sentence was never finished.

137

Something was happening on the other side of the veil. At first they were only aware of a sense of something, or someone, as though a person had entered the holy place. Then they were aware of the shadowy form of the ark of the covenant as though there were a light behind it casting its shadow onto the veil.

"Look!" Ithamar said, obviously startled. "Look! . . . the holy of holies is getting radiantly bright; we can see obscurely through the veil."

"It's the shekinah of God," Aaron said. "Light is a part of the nature of God, so, when He enters, the light of His presence fills the room. As a matter of fact it is the only light God has provided for the holy of holies. It will come to rest between the faces of the cherubim on the mercy seat."

"It's a strange sensation to stand here and watch that light increase in intensity," Eleazar said. "I don't think I can say that I am afraid but I am overawed by it, and I'm glad for the protective veil between us and it."

"Not *it,* my son," Aaron said, *"Him!* We are being allowed to watch as God enters His tabernacle. He must be calling Moses in for a time of communication."

"Don't you think we had better step out of here before Moses arrives?" Ithamar said as he started towards the doorway.

As he pulled back the drapery that formed the doorway to the outer court Ithamar saw Moses entering the eastern gate.

"Here he comes now," he said. "Just look at that determined walk of his."

Aaron and Eleazar joined Ithamar in the doorway, and watched Moses as he passed the brazen altar headed for the tabernacle. His head was bowed as though he were watching every step he took. His stride was stretched, and he put each foot down with determination.

Moses rushed past the three men as though he didn't even see them. Salutations and small talk were unimportant to him now; he had far more important things on his mind. God was calling.

138

With hardly a break in his stride Moses marched right into the holy of holies, stepped before the ark of the covenant, and bowed himself low before the Lord.

"Here I am Lord," he finally said. "What would you have me to do?"

Reverently, Aaron and his sons slipped into the outer court, letting the curtain close ever so gently.

"He marched in there like he would walk into his own tent," Ithamar said.

"Well," Aaron responded, "it is almost as familiar to him as his own tent. Not only did he get the pattern for the entire tabernacle from God but he personally constructed the ark of the covenant (Deut. 10:3) to be the container of the two tables of stone upon which God wrote the commandments the second time. It was the first piece of furniture that God described, and was constructed before Bezaleel was anointed to oversee the construction of the tabernacle. Later on, Bezaleel overlaid the ark inside and out with pure gold" (Exod. 25:11).

"It really isn't very big, is it?" Ithamar asked.

"It's less than half the size of the brazen altar," Eleazar volunteered, "about two and a half cubits long (four feet) by one and a half cubits wide (two and a half feet). It stands exactly the same height as the table of shewbread, one and a half cubits, which connects God's throne with our table of fellowship."

"These half measures are unique to the tabernacle, aren't they?" Ithamar asked. "Nothing else is 'cut in two' as this Hebrew word suggests."

"Nothing except the height of our table," Eleazar said.

"But why?" Ithamar asked.

"Well," Aaron said, "three becomes one and a half when we cut it into two parts, and three is the number of manifestation and of our God. This earthly throne of His can only half manifest His gloriousness. Here we three are already afraid of the time we will have to approach even half a revelation of God; what would it be like if He were to fully reveal himself to us there on His throne?''

"If you're going to deal with divine numerology," Ithamar said, "what about that two and a half cubits length? Isn't that half of five which speaks of divine grace? After all God has done for us in leading us out of Egypt and into this special relationship with himself as His covenant people how can we accept that this is only half a demonstration of grace?''

"I agree with you, son," Aaron answered, "that we have received much grace from God. But everything we have enjoyed of His great favor is in our time dimension. It has a beginning and an ending. God's full grace is eternal, without beginning or ending. We see but a fraction of His grace here on earth.''

By now the men had reached the brazen altar where Eleazar routinely picked up the brass poker and idly stoked the smoldering fire.

"I can't believe the boldness of Moses," he said as he added more wood to the fresh flames. "I'm still terrorized at the thought that someday I'll have to go in there, and yet he marched in with great anticipation.''

"Yes, I covet that," Aaron answered. "Still we must remember that we are priests unto our God while he is a friend of God (Exod. 33:11). We only see shadows and types but he sees face to face (Deut. 34:10). While we are concerned with rites and ritual, Moses is involved in a personal relationship with God (Num. 12:6-8). He has seen God, we've only seen the fire of God. As you well know, with relationship comes special privilege, and, with these intimate privileges, comes unique boldness. Many in Israel fear to approach me because I am their high priest, and yet you two are very comfortable around me.''

"But you don't seem like a high priest to us; you're our father," Ithamar said.

"And that's the way Moses feels about God," Aaron said. As an appointed priest, Aaron almost dreaded entering God's presence, yet as a friend of God, Moses delighted in it.

Of course it would be several centuries before either this "son-priest" relationship or the "friend-of-God" relationship would be widely available, but now that the Aaronic priesthood has been totally replaced by the priesthood of Christ, a penitent seeker after God at the cross can become a priest unto the most high God by being born into the family of Christ (John 1:12). Furthermore, since Christ came, suffered, and died for our justification (Rom. 4:25) we have been made a "kingdom of priests" (1 Pet. 2:9; Rev. 1:6) with access rights to the throne, for Paul wrote, "Through him [Christ] we . . . have access . . . unto the Father" (Eph. 2:18) and "In whom we have . . . access with confidence by the faith of him (Eph. 3:12).

As a result of the new birth, we become priests by lineage, son-priests, as were Aaron's sons; through faith we become believer-priests, somewhat akin to the Levites, but by personal and intimate relationship with God we become friend-priests whose throne rights are based upon relationship to God, rather than through lineage or office, very much like Moses.

Toward the end of Christ's earthly relationship with the eleven faithful disciples He told them: "Ye are my friends . . . henceforth I call you not servants; for the servant knoweth not what his lord doeth: but I have called you friends" (John 15:14-15). So the New Testament saint has access to the holy of holies by lineage, by faith, and by an intimate relationship. Perhaps this explains why we have been urged to "come boldly unto the throne of grace, that we may obtain mercy, and find grace to help in time of need" (Heb. 4:16). The fearful approach of the Old Testament priest has been replaced by the fearless and faith-filled approach of the New Testament priest.

Since no man in the Old Testament, including Moses, had more right to God's throne than an obedient New Testament believer-priest has, we are challenged: "Having therefore, brethren, boldness to enter into the holiest by the blood of Jesus, by a new and living way, which he hath consecrated for us, through the veil, that is to say, his flesh. . . . Let us draw near with a true heart in full assurance of faith, having our hearts sprinkled from an evil conscience, and our bodies washed with pure water" (Heb. 10:19, 20, 22).

This "new and living way" does not replace the tabernacle approach, it fulfills it. We come first "by the blood of Jesus," (Heb. 10:19) which answers to the brazen altar. Next we come "with a true heart" (Heb. 10:22) which answers to the inspection and cleansing done at the laver. Our third step is "full assurance of faith" (Heb. 10:22) which answers to the illumination of the lampstand and the Holy Spirit's "gift of faith" (1 Cor. 12:9) and is the central authority for our approach because, "without faith it is impossible to please him; for he that cometh to God must believe that he is, and that he is a rewarder of them that diligently seek him" (Heb. 11:6).

Our fourth preparatory step is listed as, "having our hearts sprinkled" (Heb. 10:22), which beautifully answers to the table of shewbread where frankincense was sprinkled on the shewbread which had been placed upon the golden table. It speaks of the removal of all condemnation by accepting heaven's sweet fragrance of forgiveness upon our lives. Through "the glory of his grace . . . he hath made us accepted in the beloved" (Eph. 1:6).

The final act of preparation refers to the special cleansing given to the high priest on the Day of Atonement—our bodies washed with pure water. The believer-priest is offered a victorious life in addition to the vicarious cleansings of Christ's work. The inner nature is cleansed and the outer practice is changed so that he genuinely becomes a new creation, who dares to enter into the presence of God unashamedly and unafraid.

So as surely as Moses walked confidently and expectantly into God's chamber we, too, as believer-priests and friends of God, dare to come through the veil, which Hebrews calls the flesh of Christ (10:20), knowing that it was torn open from the top to the bottom (by the hand of God) when Jesus died on the cross (Matt.

27:51). There is, indeed, a new and a living way opened for us to approach God. But what Moses saw would differ from what we see only to the extent that a type differs from its antitype or a model differs from the completed building. The scene is accurate but the scope is small.

As New Testament friends of God and priests unto the Most High God through the lineage of Christ Jesus, let's step through the veil and stand alongside of Moses as he bows before the ark of the Lord. It won't startle him for on the Mount of Transfiguration he and Christ discussed the ramifications of the cross (Luke 9:30-31), which includes our right of entrance. He understands the New Testament priest's position in the heavenlies quite thoroughly. We won't interrupt Moses though God has finished speaking. Neither of them seems eager to leave. The glow of God's shekinah still fills the room with a warm, shadowless light that has a quality of peacefulness to it. There is no questioning that this is indeed the throne of God before which we stand.

Without so much as acknowledging our presence Moses said, "You realize, of course, that this ark typifies the person of the Lord Jesus Christ. All of the other items of furniture outside of this room speak of His work. The previous two arks, the one that preserved Noah and his family, and the one that spared me as a baby, also spoke of Christ but are generally remembered more for what they did than for what they were.

"This ark, made of wood and gold is here to reveal the person of Christ far more than the purpose of Christ," he continued. "The Father beholds who His Son is before viewing what His Son has done. It is the ark (His person) that supports the mercy seat (His work).

"How sad the Father must feel to see most New Testament saints choose to revel in Christ's work rather than rejoice in His person," Moses added. "They memorialize the cross rather than Him who died upon it." A man, a New Testament saint, joins Moses in the holy of holies at this point.

"You are right, Moses," the New Testament saint said. "We are very much like Aaron and his sons for we too spend most of our lives in the outer court serving the needs of the people, and seeing the provision of Jesus in the cross and in the word as the only answer to these needs. Still we would have to confess that this is not the way the New Testament reveals Christ. John the Baptist announced: 'Behold the Lamb of God [His person], which taketh away [His work] the sin of the world' (John 1:29). Paul expressed it: 'I determined not to know any thing among you, save Jesus Christ [His person], and him crucified' [His work] (1 Cor. 2:2). Similarly the Book of Revelation declares: 'I beheld . . . and in the midst of the elders, stood a Lamb [His person] as it had been slain' [His work] (5:6). So the New Testament reveals His person first and His work second just as the Father sees Him in here."

Moses nodded his head in assent. "God always gives His perspective when He speaks but His words are usually translated according to our personal needs," he said.

"For example," Moses continues, "God views the tabernacle as His means of abiding with men while we view it as our means of getting in to God. God dwells here at His throne, and flows out to us in the outer court while we begin our approach out at the brazen altar, and work our way in to God's throne. For although this is God's room and His furniture, its purpose is to provide a meeting place where God and man can get together. Naturally we will first view the work of Jesus before seeing His office for until His ministry has performed changes in us we are unable to draw near enough to God's holy place to behold the perfections of Christ's person."

"This is true, Moses," saint said, "but isn't it equally true that His works reveal His person just as His person contains His works?"

"What do you mean by 'His person contains His works?' " Moses asked.

"Who He is makes possible what He does. The works are

144

always in the workman. For instance, Moses, what does this ark contain?''

''The two tables of stone on which God wrote His covenant,'' Moses said, ''and a pot of manna. I put them in there myself.''

''Yes,'' saint answered, ''that's all that is in the ark right now, and only the tables of stone will remain in the ark when it is the solitary piece of tabernacle furniture to be transferred into Solomon's temple in Jerusalem (1 Kings 8:9). But from my New Testament perspective I know that very shortly you will be adding another item to the ark, Aaron's rod that budded (Heb. 9:4).

Taking saint firmly by the arm Moses led him a few steps towards the veil as he said, ''Explain that to me, please. You are talking about something that has not yet happened to me.''

''I realize that,'' saint said, ''but in principle, it already has. Before long many in Israel will join Korah in an insurrection against you and Aaron. They will attempt to overthrow the Aaronic line. God will tell the head of each tribe to cut a rod, symbol of authority, and put his name on it. You will lay all twelve rods before the Lord overnight, and all but Aaron's rod will wither and die, while his will not only stay green but will blossom, bud and bear fresh almonds, proving once and for all that the question of the priesthood is to be determined solely by Jehovah! No volunteers, no elections, only divine appointments.''

''This I can understand. But why would God feel this incident important enough to have me place the rod inside the ark?'' Moses asked.

''Because it is such a fitting type of Jesus who was totally rejected by men both as a prophet and a priest. Although they cut Him off at the cross God resurrected Him giving Him instant fruitfulness.''

''That's absolutely beautiful,'' Moses said, stroking his beard as though that would help the truth to soak in faster. ''And it is so consistent with His gracious nature,'' he added.

By this time saint had learned that although Moses is best known as the law-giver, he had been given great glimpses into God's grace. Repeatedly he would see God make gracious provision for man to avert divine punishment.

"Did you say that, after the promised land has been conquered and a permanent dwelling place for God has been built, the pot of manna and Aaron's rod will be removed from the ark?" Moses asked.

"Yes, Moses," saint said. "These items are concerned with God's people during their earthly wanderings. However, God's word will be as active when the redeemed are at rest in heaven as it is while they are on trek here on earth."

"As you well know," Moses said, "the ark was originally made as a repository of the covenant. When I broke the first two tables of stone God realized that no man could keep His law so He instructed me to build a wooden ark of these half dimensions, and placed His law therein. It is in the man Christ Jesus that God has deposited His laws. Only He can keep them unbroken."

"Oh, how right you are," saint said. "Since no man can keep God's law, God made a man who could keep it. After Jesus had perfectly kept those commandments He was covered with divine glory just as you overlaid this wooden ark with gold after the law had been placed in it."

"Are you suggesting," Moses asked, "that Jesus Christ keeps God's law representatively just as our ark keeps the law emblematically?"

"Precisely so," saint answered. "God's word tells us, 'by the obedience of one shall many be made righteous' (Rom. 5:19). Jesus Christ was the obedient one. When the Father places us in Him, He becomes our righteousness. We are declared righteous even though we are not yet performing righteousness. As surely as we cover the imperfections of small children with our love knowing that training and maturity will correct those faults, so God covers our blemishes and defects with His great mercy so that we can come into obedience."

"So your righteousness is imputed just as ours is," Moses said. "We impute our unrighteousness to an innocent animal, and receive its life imputed to us, and you do the same thing to Christ, God's Lamb."

"True," saint said. "It requires faith to make it work, though."

"So does our sacrificial system," Moses added. "Unless we believe God will do what He said He would do, our entire system is nothing but a display of religious ritual."

Finding that the principles of God are the same whether they are unveiled under the Old Covenant or the New was comforting to both Moses and saint. A feeling of comradeship began to develop between these two believers. For although one had learned these principles on the mountain in the presence of God, and the other had learned them from the Bible under the guidance of the Holy Spirit there was no conflict. While they saw things from different positions the foundation of faith in Christ was the same from both viewpoints.

"I was wondering," Moses said as he moved slowly back towards the ark, "if my close association with the law and the ark may have given me a perspective of God's word you may have overlooked. Do you realize that God's testimony is confined, concealed, and conciliated here in the ark?"

"No, I hadn't given that any thought," saint said.

"Well, consider first of all," Moses responded, "that the ark was built to contain the law. The tables were confined. The unconfined law that I brought down from the mountain the first time was violated by the people before they ever saw it. They had heard God give it orally but still couldn't keep it. Once it was broken its curses and penalties swept out over Israel and slew three thousand men."

"It has always interested me," saint interrupted, "that the first time law was preached three thousand were killed (Exod. 32:28), but the first time grace was preached, on the day of Pentecost, three thousand were saved (Acts 2:41).

147

Moses smiled knowingly. "That was possible because the word of God had been confined within the ark Christ Jesus by then. The men on the day of Pentecost were not more righteous than those who perished at the foot of Sinai. My people had only worshiped a golden calf but those people had crucified Christ, God's Son. Yet rather than slay them God forgave them. Man's only hope of mercy is for the law to be confined in Christ."

"And that confinement also becomes its concealment, doesn't it?" saint asked.

"It does when you put a lid on it," Moses answered. "Until this mercy seat was constructed the statutes were still visible. But, once Bezaleel set the golden lid on the box, the tables were hidden from view. We can get their message only when God speaks it to us from between the faces of the cherubim here on the mercy seat."

"That principle is still true," saint responded. "Although we now have a Bible that has been translated into more languages than any other piece of literature it is still both confined and concealed in Christ. The fact that we can read it doesn't mean that we can understand it.

"No matter how good a scholar we may be or how proficient we may become in the original Bible languages we cannot really know what God is saying until we come to Christ. God's book is indeed concealed in Christ, and will only be revealed through Him. To know the written word requires that we come to know the living word."

"Yes, I can see that principle," Moses said. "All the righteous demands of the law must be met, and all of its penalties must be extracted or God's justice would be greatly compromised. But in the shedding of blood all of God's justice is satisfied and His word is fulfilled. Although we deserve to be punished we are fully pardoned."

"Compared to the beauty of the mercy seat, the ark is quite plain, isn't it?" saint said.

"Plain but precious," Moses answered, "for upon the ark rests the revelation of God. It is the foundation of God's throne upon the earth. If the mercy seat were to come off we would not only have an exposed law but a dethroned God. That's why there is a crown around the top of the ark to hold the lid securely in place.''

Both men stood next to the ark silently lost in contemplation. Although the fiery burning of God's presence no longer filled the gap between the faces of the cherubim the room was still radiant with the sense of God's presence.

After what seemed like an eternity of silence, saint broke the tranquility by saying, ''There's an amazing uniqueness about this ark. It is unlike any other piece of furniture. None other forms the base for another as does the ark for the mercy seat.''

"And no other piece resides in the holy of holies," Moses added.

"Or will ever be taken out of the tabernacle for use as the ark will'' (1 Sam. 4:3-4), saint said.

"Nor do any of the other items of furniture have such multiple purposes or uses as this ark does," Moses said.

"How's that?" saint asked.

"For instance," Moses said, "this ark is the seat of government for Israel. We are a theocracy. God is the head of our government ruling our affairs through me, the priests, and the elders. All of our instructions come from God's throne.''

"Oh yes," saint said, "it is still very much that way. Christ is the head of the church, and He gave apostles, prophets, evangelists, pastors, and teachers to implement His reign.''

"Still a second use for the ark is communication," Moses said. "God clearly said that He would speak to us from between the cherubim (Exod. 25:22). All of His instructions are transmitted to us from the top of the ark.''

"God still communicates through the ark," saint said. 'God, who at sundry times and in divers manners spake in time past unto the fathers by the prophets, hath in these last days spoken unto us by his Son . . .' '' (Heb. 1:1-2).

"And do you get your guidance from the ark?" Moses asked. "Israel never moves out of the camp until the ark leads the way. We've never been this way before so we desperately need a guide."

"Most certainly we are led by the ark, Christ Jesus," saint said. "He is our example, our pattern, our forerunner, and He gave each believer a deposit of His Spirit so that we can be led both subjectively and objectively."

"There is still another use God has provided for this ark. When we enter the land we are to carry the ark into the battle. As long as God is leading the battle we will win, but if we go in our strength and try to engage the enemy in our own wisdom we will be defeated," Moses said.

"How we New Testament believers need to be reminded of this," saint said. "We dare not enter any conflict that Christ has not led us into. Knowing our spiritual enemy and how to use our spiritual weapons does not give us license to start a battle. Christ is the commander in chief, and He will engage the enemy in battle in His own time, using His methods and employing His weapons. We must learn to take orders not to try to give them. Yes, Christ is the key to all of our victories. Every action of our flesh produces failure and disaster. It is only when the ark is leading that we enjoy spiritual victory."

"Blessed is this ark of God which governs, communicates, guides, and guarantees victory to the church. How imperative it is that the church draw near the ark regularly," saint concluded.

"But if the ark, which forms the foundation, is so blessed, how much more blessed must the crowning mercy seat be?" Moses asked. "Just look at its massive beauty and try to calculate its worth."

150

THE MERCY SEAT.

CHAPTER 10

The Mercy Seat
EXODUS 25:17-22

Saint stared at the glistening gold of the mercy seat. Although the very walls of the room were covered with gold, this massive piece of solid gold, which had been beaten into shape by the skillful artistry of Bezaleel, captivated his attention. The delicate work on the two cherubim, who faced each other on the top of this lid with their wings outstretched forming a protective shield over the lid, intrigued saint thoroughly. They looked so lifelike he almost expected them to lift their faces from their downward view and look at him.

"This is the ultimate piece of furniture," Moses explained. All other pieces point to it, and all other ministries prepare us for it. There is nothing higher available to us here on earth for this is God's propitiatory; His mercy seat; His throne; His judgment seat, and His place of communion with man.

"What a pair they make," Moses went on, pointing to the ark and the mercy seat. Once joined they are never to be separated. The person of Christ and the propitiatory of God are one and the same, but in the revelation of His person He was wood overlaid with gold (the God-man) while in the revelation of God's propitiatory it is solid gold. Man can contribute nothing to his redemption. It depends wholly and absolutely on God. There is no wood (man) in God's mercy seat. It is all divine glory (gold)."

"Not only is it gold," saint added, "but it is beaten gold, very much like the lampstand. Everything on the mercy seat was formed from one solid piece of gold, even the two cherubs."

"It had to be done that way," Moses said, "to keep from violating the type. This mercy seat is a type of Christ in His highest revelation for it shows Christ in His relationship to God the Father. His unique oneness with the Father and singleness of purpose in accomplishing His will dared not be compromised by making this seat in sections."

"Of course not," saint said. "And the only way to do this was by using the hammer. What a picture of the sufferings of Jesus Christ as God formed Him into a propitiatory."

"Does your generation, which has never known the sacrificial system, understand the meaning of propitiation, and how that differs from the propitiatory?" Moses asked.

"I believe so," saint answered, "for just a few years ago America launched one of its men into orbit around the earth in a rocket powered spaceship. Since he was the first man to ever leave our atmosphere we were justly apprehensive about his reentry. We had watched meteorites completely burn out as they fell into our atmosphere, and wondered if a man-made object could withstand the tremendous heat caused by the friction. Our fears were heightened when we lost all radio contact with him as he entered the ionosphere. Not knowing that this was a normal phenomenon we feared that the capsule had already disintegrated. You can imagine the relief of thousands of Americans as radio communications were reestablished with John Glenn. When mission control asked John how seriously the heat was building up he replied, 'the propitiatory shield is doing its work. I am fine.'

"He was talking about a huge dish-like shield that had been built onto the bottom of the capsule," saint continued. "Upon reentry the ship had been turned around so that the heat shield would penetrate the earth's atmosphere first. It heated white hot, and much of it burned away, but it took the heat that the capsule would have taken if the shield had not been there. It was the propitiatory, but when it accepted the heat in the place of the capsule, it was a propitiation.''

"Frankly I don't know what you are talking about," Moses said. "You obviously have your modern inventions but we have our divine institutions. We know that 'to propitiate' signifies to appease, to placate, to make satisfaction. We see propitiation being made in the death of the sacrificial animals at the brazen altar. It is there, as God's bleeding Lamb, that Christ becomes our propitiation. He accepts God's wrath and placates the righteous demands of the law. But it is at the mercy seat, where God is at rest, that Christ is viewed as the propitiatory. Here His person is seen, or, as you explained it, here He is the shield. Out at the brazen altar His work is seen, just as your shield did its work upon reentry. Propitiation is the work done to appease God while the propitiatory is that which did the appeasing.''

"So," saint added, "it was at the cross that propitiation was effected but it is at the mercy seat, the propitiatory, that the abiding value of Christ's sacrifice is constantly attested to. Paul told us: 'Being justified freely by his grace through the redemption that is in Christ Jesus: whom God hath set forth to be a propitiation [better, a propitiatory] through faith in his blood, to declare his righteousness for the remission of sins that are past' (Rom. 3:24-25). The Greek word translated here as 'propitiation' is the same word translated 'mercy seat' in Hebrews 9:5 so we are convinced that God is declaring that Christ is the propitiatory as a constant declaration that sins of the past have been paid in full.''

"I like that," Moses said. "Too often people see the propitiation of Christ as merely a covering or a pardoning. But actually through the blood we are completely justified (Rom. 3:24). To accomplish this the price of sin must be paid in full.''

"Oh, yes," saint said. "Man became bankrupt through sin. At

Calvary, God did not try to extract even more from a bankrupt person, but Jesus Christ, who had gone surety for our debts, paid in full. So because of the action of a guarantor, the bankrupt was set free without in any way taking one thing away from the creditor.''

"And God is constantly reminded that all past debts have been paid in full by using the propitiatory as His throne,'' Moses said. "He did not choose to abide on the brazen altar for that would have been too threatening to men. Instead He dwells on the mercy seat which has been made a propitiatory.''

"So as the propitiatory we see Christ as man's redeemer,'' saint said.

"Yes,'' Moses answered, "and as the mercy seat we view Him as the creator.''

"How do you see that in the mercy seat?'' saint asked.

"The seat shows God at rest. It is the only chair in the entire tabernacle,'' Moses said. "Since the work of the priests was never completed, no place of rest was provided for them in the tabernacle. They had a table but no chairs. But at the end of creation God rested on the seventh day.''

"This is equally true of the new creation work of God,'' saint said. "After Christ, our high priest, offered himself as the permanent sin sacrifice, He 'sat down on the right hand of the Majesty on high' '' (Heb. 1:3).

"How wonderfully reassuring it is to know that God is not feverishly striving to redeem men and re-create them into His own image,'' Moses said. "He is so convinced that His plan cannot fail that He has seated himself as a spectator just watching the process work.''

"If I hadn't read that same thing in the New Testament I would probably disagree with you,'' saint said. "It says, 'But this man [Jesus], after he had offered one sacrifice for sins for ever, sat down on the right hand of God; from henceforth expecting till his enemies be made his footstool. For by one offering he hath perfected for ever them that are sanctified' '' (Heb. 10:12-14).

"Yes," Moses said, "He promised not to threaten us with great interventions into our lives, as He did from the mountain top. He promised instead to dwell here in the holy of holies, and to be available to us. This seat is His dwelling place. He inhabits the space between the faces of the cherubim."

Moses broke eye contact with saint and turned his head to again view the cherubim. Fixing his eyes on the space between their downturned faces he said, most reverently, "I well remember the words Jehovah spoke to me that day on the mountain after the people had worshiped the golden calf. Instead of condemning words, He spoke these comforting words: 'I will set my tabernacle among you: and my soul shall not abhor you. And I will walk among you, and will be your God, and ye shall be my people' " (Lev. 26:11-12).

Moses dropped his head in reverence, extended his hands straight forward with the palms upturned, and worshiped. After a period of silent meditation he began to gently sing the song he had composed after the successful crossing of the Red Sea.

> The LORD is my strength and song,
> And he is become my salvation:
> He is my God, and I will prepare him an habitation;
> My father's God and I will exalt him.
> Who is like unto thee, O LORD, among the gods?
> Who is like thee,
> Glorious in holiness, fearful in praises,
> Doing wonders, who is like unto thee?

"How such a holy God can dwell among such unholy people will always be somewhat of a mystery to me," saint said.

"And to all of us," Moses admitted. "If it were not for the blood He could not remain in our midst for very long. But His seat, this throne, is blood sprinkled. Annually, on the Day of Atonement, the high priest will bring a basin of the blood of the sin-sacrifice, and sprinkle it with his finger once on this seat and seven times on the floor in front of the mercy seat" (Lev. 16:14).

"Here at the mercy seat it becomes obvious that God entirely set us aside and acted *for himself* in saving us. It is His blood sprinkled on His throne in His heaven by His high priest that has purged our sins and provided our salvation. Our works, our ways, our feelings, and our failings have nothing to do with it."

"You've seen the atonement quite clearly," Moses told saint. "Obviously, since sin began in the heavens with Lucifer's self-exaltation it must be the heavens that are first purged by the sprinkling of blood. One sprinkling is enough to satisfy God. The remainder of the blood is sprinkled on the earth before the mercy seat. This is the ground you and I stand on when we come into the presence of the living God. We are so prone to doubt that God gives a sevenfold sprinkling as a complete testimony to us that we stand on safe ground before the ark of the Lord."

"Seven is the number of perfectness," saint added. "It is a perfect assurance of our rights before God. But I wonder, Moses, if it might also speak of a sevenfold perfecting of the man who comes before God. Is it not true that we are enabled to make fresh appropriation of the blood when standing in His holy presence? In spite of all of the cleansings of the outer court are there not still areas of our inner lives that need faith's appropriation of the purging blood?"

"Most certainly," Moses said. "Our evil hearts of unbelief, our seared consciences, our prideful hearts, and the vain imaginations of our minds all need repeated applications of the blood. This we do by faith's appropriation when standing worshipfully in God's presence."

"What a blessed blood-soaked mercy seat!" saint said.

"Amen," Moses said. "But remember that this seat is also His throne. He who esteems the blood also embraces the scepter. He who is seen as the redeemer at the propitiatory, and creator at the mercy seat, is also revealed as the king on His throne."

"Yes," saint concurred, "Christ died to place God's throne among us. Once God's righteousness was vindicated His reign was fully vouchsafed. His governmental authority is automatically extended over all who come to Him by virtue of the blood. Paul even taught that the essence of salvation is in confessing the lordship of Jesus (Rom. 10:9-10). Jesus proclaimed the kingdom of God, and was both born and crucified as Israel's king" (Matt. 2:2; 27:37).

Moses nodded his head approvingly. "God sits on this throne in governmental authority, but He also exercises judgment from it. If we submit to His reign we do not face Him as our judge, but every insurrectionist will stand before the judgment seat, for God's laws must be obeyed or their penalities will be enforced."

"It almost seems inconsistent to call this a judgment seat after seeing it as the mercy seat," saint said.

"Ah," Moses said, "God's mercy cannot extend beyond His laws. To illustrate this, tell me the dimensions of this seat."

"Well, since it is a lid for the ark it has to be the same size in length and width."

"Exactly," Moses said. "God's mercy seat totally covers His law, but no more. Any time man attempts to extend God's grace beyond the boundaries of His law he is headed for disgrace. Our liberty in Christ can never become a license to sin."

"Yes, I understand that," saint said, "for the New Testament consistently speaks of God being 'just and the justifier' (Rom. 3:26). He can only justify to the limits that the blood has purchased justice."

"True," Moses said, "but I noticed when you gave me the dimensions of this seat you failed to give me its height."

"We New Testament believers do not know how high it is for God didn't record this dimension anywhere in His word," saint answered.

"That's right," Moses said. "But do you realize why?"

"I used to puzzle over that," saint said, "until one day I read: 'For as the heaven is high above the earth, so great is his mercy toward them that fear him' (Psa. 103:11). Then I realized that although God's mercy cannot go beyond His word there is a height to it that is incalculable.''

"If you still feel it is inconsistent to refer to this seat as a judgment seat,'' Moses said, "I urge you to take a good look at its ornamentation. What do you see?''

"Beautiful cherubs facing each other with outstretched wings and bowed heads. Bezaleel did a masterful job in making them one with the rest of the lid,'' saint said.

"I agree,'' Moses said. "The cherubs are beautifully done. But what do they speak of to you?''

"Since the first time we read about them in Scripture is when God thrust Adam and Eve out of the garden because of their sin and placed cherubim with flaming swords to guard the way to the tree of life, I've always associated them with the administration of God's justice,'' saint said.

"You're right,'' Moses said, "for that seems to be their specific ministry. Would not their presence here on the mercy seat indicate that they are guarding and administering God's justice? God's justice and His mercy are inseparable. They are one piece just as this lid is one piece.

"Fortunately, however, the cherubs are not looking at God's law, which they know so well, but are looking at the sprinkled blood which they find hard to understand'' (1 Pet. 1:11-12), Moses continued. "They do not stand with flaming swords prohibiting our coming to the source of life, they stand with extended wings providing covering over the entire ark of the covenant. They are involved with the judicial holiness of God but are interested in the unfolding of God's redemptive plan. They are agents of judgment and yet students of His mercy.''

"I'm so thankful that my sin has been judged in Christ already,'' saint said. "I do not approach this as a judgment seat but as a mercy seat. I'm grateful that the law is covered by this golden throne, and that it has been sprinkled with blood. Yet I realize that those who do not come to the cross for judgment of sin must come to the throne for it.''

"It's a throne of grace any day that we approach it the blood sprinkled way," Moses said. "For God has designated this throne as the place He would meet with man. He specifically said: 'There I will meet with thee, and I will commune with thee from above the mercy seat, from between the two cherubims which are upon the ark of the testimony' (Exod. 25:22). This is His place of appointment—'there I will meet with thee.' ''

"In a very real sense," saint said, "we meet Jesus at the brazen altar, and the Holy Spirit at the lampstand, but it is at the propitiatory that we meet and commune with God.''

"True," Moses said. "And we have the table in the holy place for communion with the priests but it is here at the mercy seat that we have communion with Father God. We know that communion and communication with redeemed man is God's ultimate purpose in redemption. From Adam through Enoch, Noah, Abraham, and now in my own life experience, God has longed for fellowship with man. This tabernacle has not been designed and constructed merely to deal with man's sin, but to restore man to fellowship with His God. The putting away of sin is merely a necessary means to an end. God will do whatever is necessary to change man back into a creature that enjoys His presence, and is capable of responding to Him. And this ultimate purpose of God is realized here at this ultimate piece of furniture—the meeting place.''

As Moses was talking the light in the room gradually increased in intensity until what appeared to be a fireball entered at the ceiling level close to the veil, and slowly moved towards the mercy seat. As it took its position between the faces of the cherubim, saint felt such a glow of love that he wanted to embrace the entire mercy seat including the glowing demonstration of God's presence. He was nearly transfixed as he stared at the light knowing that God had reentered the room.

Moses, who was accustomed to God's presence, had already prostrated himself on the floor with his hands extended towards the ark.

Saint lost little time in joining him in this posture of adoration. Although he couldn't see anything in this prone position he could feel plenty. He was very aware of the divine presence and somewhat overawed by it; yet he was unafraid. There was a warm glow of ecstasy flowing through him, and he was aware of being surrounded by truth even though he heard no words being spoken. However, as saint grew more accustomed to his physical and emotional reactions to God's presence, his spiritual sensitivity sharpened to the point that he could discern the voice of God gently speaking.

The voice said: "Behold, the tabernacle of God is with men, and he will dwell with them, and they shall be his people, and God himself shall be with them, and be their God" (Rev. 21:3). And God further said: "I am Alpha and Omega, the beginning and the end. I will give unto him that is athirst of the fountain of the water of life freely. He that overcometh shall inherit all things: and I will be his God, and he shall be my son" (Rev. 21:6-7).

This was more than saint could handle emotionally. Lifting himself to his knees and raising his hands and face he cried: "Alleluia; Salvation, and glory, and honour, and power, unto the Lord our God . . . Alleluia, amen" (Rev. 19:1, 3).

Moses lifted his face and looked at saint reprovingly.

But again the voice from between the faces of the cherubim spoke, saying: "Praise our God, all ye his servants, and ye that fear him, both small and great" (Rev. 19:5).

That was good enough for Moses. Raising himself to his knees alongside of saint the two of them chanted in unison: "Thou art worthy, O Lord, to receive glory and honour and power: for thou hast created all things, and for thy pleasure they are and were created" (Rev. 4:11). "Blessing, and honour, and glory, and power, be unto him that sitteth upon the throne" (Rev. 5:13).

From the throne came the voice of God again, saying: "The Spirit and the bride say, Come. And let him that heareth say,

Come. And let him that is athirst come . . ." (Rev. 22:17).

And down through the centuries of time the voices of multiplied thousands of believers have responded to this invitation with the cry: *"Let us draw near* with a true heart . . ." (Heb. 10:22, italics mine).

CHAPTER 11

The Epilogue

But these crying voices have been silenced again and again by apostasy and religious regulations.

In the days of Samuel the priesthood was so corrupt that God actually allowed His ark to be removed from the holy of holies and captured by the Philistines (1 Sam. 4:3). God slew the sons of Eli, Israel's high priest, in that battle, and took Eli's life the same day (1 Sam. 4:11-18). However, God had His Samuel to tend the lampstand.

It was not until the days of David that the ark was returned (2 Sam. 6:16) but by then all other articles of worship were in disuse.

Later, Solomon, David's son, built a temple as a replacement for the tabernacle but the only piece of original furniture he brought into it was the ark (2 Chron. 5:7).

And even this magnificent temple was ignored and allowed to deteriorate until young King Josiah rebuilt it and reestablished divine worship (2 Chron. 34:8).

Amazingly, the human heart quickly contents itself with something short of God, and devises elaborate substitutes for Him. God's simple route of approach is replaced by man's complex rites of religion. Repentance is replaced by penance; cleansing is replaced by ceremony; substitutional sacrifice is replaced by institutional service, and coming to church replaces coming to God.

Whether it is man's innate fear of approaching God, or religion's ingrained reluctance to allow man the freedom to attain such an intimate relationship with God is debatable, but the result is the same: man and God are separated.

This approach to God largely disappeared from the church so that during the Middle Ages, indulgences were sold as a means of cleansing from sin. It appeared that the light of God had nearly gone out, but in the early sixteenth century God successfully broke through to Martin Luther with the electrifying truth: "The just shall live by his faith" (Hab. 2:4). Within a few years the ministry of the brazen altar was restored to the church, but not without great persecution.

In the eighteenth century, God restored the ministry of the laver through the dynamic preaching of sanctification by the Wesley brothers. They, too, paid a great price as their religious brethren rejected first their message and then the men. But the church now had a complete outer court, and she contented herself in those ministries for nearly a hundred years.

But at the beginning of the twentieth century, God again visited His church with an outpouring of His Spirit that stirred the religious world. Rejection and reprisals slowly forced these Spirit-baptized saints out of their fundamental churches to form the Pentecostal denomination where the ministry of the candlestick was relearned and returned to the church. This brought a great company of believers out of the outer court into the holy place, and many of them, as had the Lutherans and the Methodists before them, felt that they had attained the ultimate in relationship with God. But, in fact, they were only at the first station inside the holy place. God still wanted a more intimate relationship with His people.

166

So, in the years following World War II, there came an additional pouring out of God's Spirit—this time "upon all flesh" (Joel 2:28). Many fundamental and historic churches were completely rejuvenated, and thousands of Catholics were introduced to the high priestly ministry of the Lord Jesus Christ. At first it was viewed as a second Pentecost but it soon became evident that this visitation was not centered around the lampstand but around the golden table of shewbread. Fellowship has been the keynote of the charismatic renewal. Denominational walls have been ignored as Spirit-filled believers gathered in conferences, prayer fellowships, and retreat centers just to enjoy Jesus and one another. Much emphasis has been placed on teaching. So great has been the hunger for the shewbread that a charismatic publishing house was born, and soon soared close to the top in the publication and sale of religious books. A national newspaper was founded, and scores of magazines have grown out of this visitation. At least two major, and a few minor television networks were formed to share the testimony, fellowship, and teaching that this golden table affords. Tape libraries, both audio and video, have sprung up all over the nation, and charismatic radio stations are very common.

So far there has not been sufficient persecution to force the formation of another denomination. It remains an open fellowship of believers. Episcopal and Catholic priests minister freely at the same conference, while Mennonites and Methodists join in singing, "Hallelujah."

It is a fellowship of believers based upon the unity of the Spirit rather than a unity of the faith. Once these believer-priests finish this time of fellowship they return to their separate stations of religious service without condemning their fellow priests for ministering in a different heritage or in a different manner. Few believed such fellowship could be enjoyed this side of heaven, but many who are enjoying it are convinced that this is the final step before heaven.

But there is still the ministry of the golden altar of incense that must be returned to the church before we step through the veil into the realized presence of God. God must bring the church beyond fellowship to pure worship. Our focus must cease to be on us and turn to Him. The thrust of activity must turn from feasting and fellowship to devotions and adoration.

Already the rays of this move are penetrating the darkness preparing the church for the full sunrise of worship. As surely as the time span between each new visitation has been shorter than the previous interval, so it appears that God will do a quick work in bringing His people from fellowship to worship. Perhaps this generation will not only move from the lampstand to the table but on to the altar of incense which is only a thin, torn veil away from the presence of God.

Maybe this is the generation of the church that: "The throne of God and of the Lamb shall be in it; and his servants shall serve him: and they shall see his face; and his name shall be in their foreheads . . . and they shall reign for ever and ever" (Rev. 22:3-5). May it be so!